# LIFE IS SAD

# &

# BEAUTIFUL

# A Prayer For Mum

I know the angel of death smiled at you when it looked left
I know the angels of Heaven are getting the keys to
unlock the gates now they hear your footsteps

I know your parents will smile when they get to hear the
calm in your voice
I know in that moment the Heavens will be notified that
the princess has arrived to rejoice

I wish all the moments we shared with you were
permanently logged
I wish they could transform to a power of love that
allows every heart you touched to be healed, even though
every heart feels robbed

My Lord, allow us to sleep peacefully when the nights
turn tough
Allow me to inform the world the lessons I learnt from
my dearest mum

Allow the kingdom she built to stand strong and keep
away the devil
Allow her flight to reach the heights of Heaven so she
can experience Heaven at every level

Allow the light of the skies to be everything she
imagined and more
Allow her giggly laugh to reach our ears from the birds
that soar
Grant us all patience to heal our delicate hearts
Grant us her presence in our futures
Even though, from this moment, she stays in our past

May the wells she planted aid the thirst of the homeless
May the du'as she prayed give hope to the hopeless
May the thousands she fed make prayers in her name
May everything I say be a copy of what she would say

My Lord, expand her grave for it to be the size of a palace
Allow every one of her good deeds to transform into
rewards that are divinely lavish

Keep her humour strong through our hardest times
Do not allow her soul to think to return when she hears
our wildest cries
Grant her the blessings in abundance within the confines
of Heaven in this everlasting afterlife

Allow her body armour to be impenetrable
For she lived a life of purity, calm, serenity; chaotic
but yet sensible

For her light so strong it took her in the night
So quick, so sudden, so blessed, so right

Have mercy on her beautiful soul
Forgive her for all she has done
And in the moment she was taken, she was taken pure
and whole

I love you forever Mother x

Ameen

Father, thank you for supporting me, for encouraging me, for allowing me to spread my wings and for giving me your blessings to fly. I love you Dad.

# Life is Sad & Beautiful

By the Original
Mummy's Boy
## Hussain Manawer

First published in Great Britain in 2022 by Yellow Kite
An imprint of Hodder & Stoughton
An Hachette UK company

3

Copyright © Hussain Manawer 2022

The right of Hussain Manawer to be identified as the
Author of the Work has been asserted by him in accordance
with the Copyright, Designs and Patents Act 1988.

Cover and internal illustrations by
Joel Robison © Hodder and Stoughton 2022
Illustration on page 294 © James Cook, typewriter artist
(@jamescookartwork & www.jamescookartwork.com)

A CIP catalogue record for this title is
available from the British Library

Hardback ISBN 978 1 529 39018 6
eBook ISBN 978 1 529 39019 3
Audiobook ISBN 978 1 529 39020 9

Typeset in Chandler42 by Goldust Design

Printed and bound in Great Britain
by Clays Ltd, Elcograf S.p.A.

Hodder & Stoughton policy is to use papers that
are natural, renewable and recyclable products and made
from wood grown in sustainable forests. The logging and
manufacturing processes are expected to conform to the
environmental regulations of the country of origin.

Yellow Kite
Hodder & Stoughton Ltd
Carmelite House
50 Victoria Embankment
London EC4Y 0DZ

www.yellowkitebooks.co.uk

'Your story and poetry is so powerful. It's going to resonate with others who haven't dealt with their grief. Thank you Hussain!'

OPRAH WINFREY, on Hussain's involvement in *The Me You Can't See* documentary series, May 2021

Rest in Peace, Power and Paradise

Ali Hussain
Jasmin Jethwa
Levi Miller
Darren Molloy-Herat
Mum

Until we meet again x

As soon as we harness our true power, we will have
enormous control over our world;

We will be able to design reality rather than merely
acting and being controlled within it.

Well-directed thought is a learnt and disciplined skill.

To manifest an intention requires a laser-like focus,
full sensory visualisation and a profound belief.

Perception has the ability to be transformed,

Ability will then have the capability to live,

And through living, your dreams ultimately have a chance
to come alive,

Then you've increased the odds and possibility is true.

*If you can make it out of your mind*
*You can make it anywhere*

# CONTENTS

# CONTENTS

# CONTENTS

None of what I do,
Nothing of what I write,
Would have ever been possible without you by my side.
You would pray for me as I tried, cried, and would write
  through the night,
You fought all my demons and brought Noor into my life
Even when you walked out,
You didn't leave with your light

Mum, I want you to know,
I finally did it;

Your son won tonight.
The words led me out of my maze,
They led me out of the episodes,
I was so shocked when they finally led me out
  of my brain.

Now, it's time to tell the world;
My name is Hussain.
A name my dear mother gave.

I kept going because that was everything that
  you prayed.

It's finally time for me to go and show the world
  exactly who my mother made.

# Preface

(still don't know what this means)

I often get asked if I always knew I wanted to be a poet. Truth be told, the answer is 'hell to the no'; I had no idea this was even an option. I studied and graduated for a degree in Quantity Surveying at the University of Westminster (*must have been the pressure of deciding on something when I was 17*). The arts were something I was truly fascinated and captivated by, but genuinely believing I could make a career out of writing down my thoughts, feelings, hurts and upsets was never something that I felt was viable or obtainable.

My grandparents came to England in 1960 and raised our family in the London Boroughs of Newham and Barking and Dagenham. My parents met twice before getting married. My dad ran a video cassette shop on Romford Road before developing the legendary Mobeen restaurant on Ilford Lane, and my mother helped him, raised us and did so much more along the way.

East London became my life: growing up with the sounds of the Hammers at Upton Park, the smells from Queen's Market on Green Street, the hustle and bustle of Ilford Lane, Vicarage Field in Barking ... they all played a pivotal role in shaping me into the man I am today. I remember being in Highlands Primary School and auditioning for the 'choir'; I must have been in Year 5. I got in (*miraculously, somehow*) and, as a collective with hundreds of school children from across the country, in 2002 I had my first ever window into the world of performing as we sang the words of *West Side Story* through the roof at the Royal Albert Hall.

There was something I found truly remarkable about rhyming words. I remember in singing assemblies I had my favourite songs - the ones I wished would get played. I also recall feeling deeply emotional every time I heard a movie soundtrack hit. And at some point during my teens I was introduced to the wonderful world of garage and grime music whilst learning Shakespeare, understanding Rumi and reading monologues, scripts and anthologies of poems.

I began writing. It was in the back of my school planner; I remember it as if it was yesterday. There was a fulfilling sensation I discovered each time I managed to release a feeling out of me onto the paper.

Skip 15 years on and here we are. Growing up as an artist meant I had to work multiple jobs throughout various stages of my life. These ranged from positions at Primark, Suits You, Curry's, Supreme O Glaze, Sainsbury's, The O2 arena, inside Shakespeare's Globe theatre, working as a television extra, and so many more in between.

Each time I would come home from a shift, tired and with my feet aching from the cheap black shoes I would be wearing, I'd run upstairs to the attic room and write down how I felt, what I saw and how people made me feel. My mother was worried - she could not understand that her son with a degree was not fulfilling it and was opting instead to choose an alternative career path, one with a vast amount of uncertainty. She would constantly ask me, 'Is it happening yet, Hussain? Is it happening?' And I would reply, 'Not yet Mum, not yet.'

It's been five long years without you Mother, and
I can finally say, 'It's happening Mum, it's really
happening.' The very sentiment of these words makes
me cry each time they begin to formulate. There is not
a day that goes by when I do not think of you, when I
don't hold you as close as I can to my heart. I've learnt
to not question the will of God and now have come to a
deeper understanding that it was your time to leave.

But it is my mother who has led me here, so no more
ramblings from me. To you, the reader, where do I begin?
Initially, when my poems first came alive, left my work
station and hit the internet, I had absolutely no idea
that this is where they would lead me. There have been
thousands and thousands of messages from people all
across the world who have connected to my words and
their meanings, and from the bottom of my heart and
art I thank each and every one of you. I thank you for
allowing these words to sit within your life and play
a role. That this is even happening is all very surreal
for me. I don't think I will ever believe it, so for
all of you who have messaged, emailed, written, shared,
liked, commented and connected, I send you the utmost
gratitude, love and light.

I apologise for the delay in getting this to you –
it's taken a lifetime, but it's all of me; there's no
getting rid of me now!

Without further ado, I present to you all, my debut
poetry book ...

*Life Is Sad and Beautiful.*

Be proud of everything you came through in life;
mentally, spiritually and psychologically
before you got to this book.

Now take off your shoes,
turn off your phone,
get comfortable;
we're going on a journey together.

Chapter One

# That Boy Just Wants to Be Heard

From my earliest memory of being a child and growing up, my mother was always asking me and my siblings to get up in front of our cousins, family members, or even just her, and recite a religious scripture or read something aloud. At first, this was a rather scary experience, as your mind would automatically go into *'What if I mess up?'*, *'What are they going to think of me?'*, *'What if I embarrass my family?'* All of these things, plus the lack of confidence, were probably the reason my mother made us do these things in the first place. I think in her eyes it was some form of preparation.

On religious gatherings we had to each pray aloud, and on family occasions when all of us cousins were in the same room, we would get up, turn by turn, and have a go at our attempt of speaking Urdu by introducing ourselves and our ages. All of this practice would ultimately prepare us each for our headline position slots at Grandma and Grandad's house on Eid.

Eid in East Ham was special: we would sit around on the floor of my grandfather's home on a large blanket, with only a few selected elders being allowed to sit on the sofa. We would have an incredible display of food, fruits, juices and desserts before us. My Baba (*my dad's father*) lay in his hospital bed in the room with us. Sadly, my Baba had a stroke and was bed-bound for the last few years of his life. But this did not stop him from enjoying mango and watermelon, communicating his best with us and feeling the energy of his vast amount of children and grandchildren in one room together.

My grandma would always pray, and before she finished her prayer she would make sure she mentioned every one of us individually. And to be real with you, I still don't know how she did it as there were so many of us. Before this and before she would close off her

prayer, we would each have to join her in a recital.
This is what Mum was really training us for - she didn't
want us to feel embarrassed. By this point, we had had
months of practice, so when it was our turn, we would
leap at the opportunity and take it with both hands.

We did well, each and every time. But that didn't
mean the practice stopped in our bedrooms before we
went to bed. We would leave our doors open and recite
our prayers aloud for each of us to hear. I would gaze
out at the stars and the moon, using the night light to
help illuminate my small prayer book and, some nights,
I would attempt the extra-long prayers. Little did I
know that these nights were to play a huge role in my
life in decades to come.

Growing up in East Ham was an incredible experience
- it was the early nineties and we lived on Central Park
Road, which is a stone's throw away from West Ham's
famous Upton Park stadium, the legendary Boleyn Cinema
(*neither of which are there now*) and down the road was
Central Park. Our time was split evenly between my
father's family in East Ham and my mother's in Barking.
One key thing about both of these areas was the local
markets: East Ham was renowned for the iconic Queen's
Market and Barking had just announced the arrival of its
new market just by Vicarage Field.

After spending many childhood years between these
two places, Dad and Mum announced to us one morning
that we would be getting a little sister. I still
remember the day my baby sister was born. I was upstairs
playing with an Action Man doll and my neighbour, who
was babysitting us at the time, ran into the room and
announced, 'Your mum has had the baby!' This was an
exceptional moment in all of our lives. Around this
time, Dad ran a video cassette shop on Romford Road and

Mum was making a living sewing clothes on her industrial sewing machine. They both worked incredibly hard.

Dad was fascinated by movies and film and was always enlightening us with stories of cinema magic and Mum was pushing us to always look smart, dress well, speak slowly and overall be good humans. Shortly after the arrival of my baby sister, Mum and her mum (my grandma) went to view a house in Ilford, Essex and came back with joyous news saying that they had found 'our new home'. I remember as a child thinking what on earth it would be like to move house and I genuinely believed we were going to pick up our home from East Ham and place it somewhere in Ilford. I never understood the concept! From then, I realised that saying goodbye was never going to be something I was good at.

A few months later, we packed our bags, had our final farewells with our neighbours, played on the climbing frame in the garden one last time and hit the road in Dad's Nissan Bluebird. Up Barking Road to the A406, get off at the Ilford exit, take the small tunnel up to Belgrave Road and say hello to your new neighbourhood - the mighty Ilford in the London Borough of Redbridge.

This semi-detached house needed a lot of work but, at the time, Mum and Dad clearly had seen a vision and wanted a better life for us away from the chaos of East Ham. There was a school down the road called Highlands Primary and that's where we would be going from now. Not only that, but each of us got our own bedroom too.

It was here one night that my life changed.

We had a small room - we called it 'the box room' - and one day my Uncle P. came round with a little machine to help us take down the old wallpaper. Once the walls were clear, the paper was in bags and out of the way,

behold, before us lay four plain blank canvases. My
older sister came up to me with a green felt-tip pen
and said, 'Let's write on the walls.' As we leaned in
closer to the plaster on the walls, I stopped and asked
her, 'What should I even write?' and she muttered to me,
'Lyrical Gangsta', and that's exactly what I did.

We stood back and admired this masterpiece. We were
so proud of ourselves, but then we heard Mum's footsteps
coming up the stairs. Petrified, we ran out of the room,
turned off the lights and acted like we were never in
there to begin with.

But in that moment, something happened, something
clicked; the sensation of writing on the wall, the
freedom of being able to flow this felt-tip pen in a
direction of my own with no limitations was special to
me. From that day on, I knew something inside me had
been sparked.

Here is my first ever piece from 2008:

# THAT BOY

*This is for all of us who spent countless nights in the
Valentines Park huts, hiding from park police, jamming
together and climbing fences. I miss that era.*

That boy just wants to be heard,
He's got a dream that nobody heard,
He was kicked, straight to the kerb,
That boy was on the edge
Just like a suburb,
That boy just wants to earn,
He's never going to quit,
He's always going to learn,
He's never going to take that, wrong turn,
  Never going to take that, wrong turn

He's never going to quit
Or stop
He doesn't want to be that high-school flop
He knows it's what he deserves
Just like a candle, when's it his time to burn?
He just needs to stick to his ambition, like glue,
But if he flops, he doesn't have a clue on what he
  would do

That boy just wants to be heard,
He's got a dream that nobody heard,
He was kicked, straight to the kerb,
  That boy was on the edge
Just like a suburb,
That boy just wants to earn,
He's never going to quit,
He's always going to learn,

He's never going to take that, wrong turn,
Never going to take that, wrong turn.

# DREAM

Once upon a time, there lived a boy called Dream
He wanted to bring night to life, and that's all what it
   seemed
When he started school he met a young girl, her name was
   Believe,
Who told him, work hard and one day you'll meet my
   cousin Achieve

Dream had a friend called Passion,
Whose brother's name was Ambition,
Whilst others studied Maths and English, they both
   studied their mission

They had cold nights and long days
And they hated this girl called Storm
Because she made them stay indoors during wet play and
   tried her best for them to meet her friend Conform

Their genuine aura kept peer pressure away with a simple
   word called Nope,
During one lesson, Dream was chilling when he met the
   new girl - her name was Hope
She said, 'Why don't you be optimistic like me, but
   don't hang yourself on that rope
'Because if you do they'll sit there and laugh just like
   what they did to the boy who left, don't you remember
   what happened to Jonathan Joke?'

As time went on they both came to realise that they both
   slept on the same page
They both had mutual friends and one of them was Mr Stage
Mr Stage was flawless; he allowed anyone to come as long
   as they entertained

One day, they got told off by an old-fashioned teacher
called Mrs Complain

Then came along Ms Talent, who said there is nothing she
would forbid,
And as seasons passed and time went on Mr Stage and Ms
Talent had a few kids

First there came Microphone, who was the loudest in the
family,
She created a lot of feedback with her brother Speaker,
but they got along happily
Then came along young Spotlight, who always shone
on others; she was always shining bright and was
reflecting the best of her brothers

Dream was getting along great,
But somehow felt uncertain
As someone stood in the way
And that someone was Mr Curtains

Hope came and said, 'Don't let Mr Curtains put you on a
pedestal,
'And when he's not looking grab your monologue and break
out of his fourth wall
'If you don't, they'll take you to the graveyard owned
by Mr and Mrs Shelf
'But if you go beyond the curtains you'll meet Mr and
Mrs Wealth'

If you have a dream in life, we can't go with you
You have to go by yourself
But when they tell you to break your leg
Just remember, you'll be in the best of health.

# DIMENSIONS

My mum told me she loved me
And it was the saddest day of my life

I had so deeply fabricated a lie within my life
I fooled myself to thinking it was right

What do you say to the woman who gave you the planet?
A galaxy to walk, a universe free from panic

The ability to walk on waterfalls, and down valued
  streams
The luxury to create memories, the memory is to dream

The bed I once laid with virgin sheets
Has me now prancing around with the devil
Who openly accepts my two left feet

He walked me in to hell and watched me build me a home
Each brick I laid with cemented sin
Coated with an elegance of chrome

My address, a handful know
And the ones who do don't wish to disclose

For there are no visitors on this taboo-infested
  district
It's real; the existence of realities beyond human
  comprehension, it's all rather mystic
The writing on the wall cannot be held liable as it
  never once cryptic
My hypothesis of flight dynamics through dimensions was
  correct, regardless of naturalistic ballistics

My mum told me she loved me
And it was the saddest day of my life

I had fallen so deep out of sight
I lost focus of what was right

But what is right?
I'm sorry for questioning
Flight controller, we have a major malfunction
The cement seems to be strengthening

No, you don't understand, you can't beat this system
It was designed, structured, built as a defence
   mechanism
Every form of resistance will increase its decision
The bricks laid on this foundation did not follow a
   tradition

What is it that you imply?
I must enter this dimension one last time
Then indulge within the prophecies of what the future
   lies
Spin through apparatus parallel to the conversion of time

So when my mum tells me she loves me
It should be the greatest day of my life

Therefore, flight controller
I am ready to take flight.

# THE PLAYGROUND

I need to fall in love with the world again
And see things the way I used to see them when I was 10
Give me nine boxes of chalk, watch me play hopscotch
A blanket and mattress and I'll make a castle and sit
   there on night watch

Put a tooth under my pillow hoping the fairy comes
   through my window
Singing b-i-n-g-o, because bingo was his name o

Give me a blue paper towel to wipe away all my worries
Mr Patel's, on a Friday to get sweets for my little tummy

Packed lunch box, a book bag, my name on a tray
Stories by Roald Dhal, the BFG would have never led me
   astray

Holding my breath, before I make my birthday wish
My Year 1 class never found Nemo, but we found the
   rainbow fish

Running through the playground, Bulldog was mental
I need to have another deep conversation with my friends
   around the classroom bin whilst sharpening my HB pencil

Let me run to the back of the coach on a school trip
It was like Dumbledore put the sorting hat on my head
   and made me feel I was chosen for this

When a nosebleed would be the worst possible disaster
And parents' evening had me scared of going home after

I really wonder if it's still there
The back of my exam desk, where I wrote 'Hussain woz 'ere'

The 'don't try this at home' never stopped me from
  wrestling
Kristian's BMX, stunt 'peds, we broke chains that's how
  fast we were peddling

The animals went in two by two, hurrah
And I'm still convinced the staff room was a secret
  hidden theme park

Discovering '21 Seconds' we all learnt how to rap
One of us jumping over the playground wall to get our
  football back

Cutting shapes with my light-up trainers, no one could
  stop me
Football stickers, Beyblades and yellow Tamagotchis

If you broke your arm, we'd graffiti the sling
You know it's going to be a mad rave when you walk into
  the hall and see a packet of party rings

You wanna see something I can do?
Give me a calculator, I'll turn it upside down, type a
  few numbers and show you how to write 'boobs'

Our paper planes glide through our classroom stratosphere
And if it hit the back of someone's head, you face the
  wall but your best mate looks at you and goes yeah

Sports day, now we're all 100-metre sprinters
Windows XP users, HP inket printers

One-hour detentions for fake parent signatures
Non-uniform days
Tracksuit wearers
Bus stop riders
Cake and custard eaters
Wet play war survivors

Sabrina was a teenage witch
Helga always bullied Arnold
Kel loved orange soda
Nobody ever won Takeshi's Castle

Ahh man I feel like my luck's up
Because I would do anything for one more game of heads
   down, thumbs up

I would mime in singing assemblies
Until I heard my favourite song
Let me lean back on my chair
Because I only learn when I'm wrong
Let me bring sherbet straws to the disco
And let me feel like a don
Let me live all the memories of the playground
Because that's where I belong
The playground where we would handle our business
The land of the young, wild, free, freaky and ambitious
Figuring out who's going to be the richest
But before that, behind the bike sheds, shirts tucked
   out, face covered in kisses

I need to fall in love with the world again
And see things the way I used to see them when I was 10
Give me nine boxes of chalk, watch me play hopscotch
A blanket and mattress and I'll make a castle and sit

there on night watch
I'll mime in singing assemblies until I hear my
  favourite song
I will lean back on my chair because I only learn when
  I'm wrong
I took sherbet straws to the disco because that made me
  feel like a don
But never in my life would I ever forget the memories of
  the playground
  As that is where we really belong.

# LEAVING HIGH SCHOOL :'(

*I wrote this poem listening to Celine Dion's 'My Heart Will Go On'.*

We were all raised on good faith
With hearts made of stealth
Five years we been together, from today once we leave the
  school gates
We will be all by ourselves

In my life I will never forget the day we all first met
I was looking to make new friends
I was looking to see what's next

With my backpack the size of a suitcase
Struggling to balance whilst sliding down the school
  staircase
No-one overly keen to get up in the assembly to showcase
The inner rapper, singer in them, that lowkey we would've
  embraced

I guess, if our paths don't cross again
I will never forget this day
Man, I'm scared to change
And I'm scared to shift my ways

Five years is like a lifetime
That we have all been here
In that time, there's moments we count
That taught us not to fear

When you reflect upon your life
You'll feel the memories of the school grounds

The running through the corridors,
The beauty of the sounds

Our lives are going to be different from today
My stars will disappear
But wherever the road takes you on your travels
Once you've settled down, you'll realise
You've never really left here

Promises will be made
Tears will be cried
We're going to keep in touch forever and ever
But I know your going to lie

In my heart we're together forever
Until the end of my line
The years we spent together
I cherish as the truest memories of our time

From English to Maths
Maths to PE
PE to Science
The laboratory
From Drama to Spanish
Spanish to French
The field days to the park bench

I remember the day I had my first sulk
I remember the time I scored my first goal
I remember the time I was first in the gym
I remember the time I climbed my first rope

I remember the day I walked through them doors
I remember the day my heart saw yours

I remember the times I would be like no more
And I remember them days I would settle the score

I remember the football matches we lost
Cross country in the park
The trampoline club after school
The oil and pastel paintings that really lit our inner
  spark

The gymnastics we could never do
Fractions that never really added up
Poetry we never got
The bleep test that never showed us any love

I remember the school trips on the coaches
Our uniform had to be tidy
As we were representatives of the school
So I pulled my best friends tie beside me

I remember the invigilators of exams
Who took their job way too seriously
I remember the myths behind many things I never got
That still live as school legends mysteriously

Parents evening was funny
That's when we put our drama skills to use
Sitting with our parents in front of our teachers
Tolerating the lies that they produced

The good teacher shone bright
Like a diamond in the staff room
We've all got the ones we never liked
And always made sure we ran past when passing their
  classrooms

I guess every so often, I do reflect upon my life
I feel the memories of the school grounds
The running through the corridors
The beauty of the sounds

Our lives are going to be different from today
My stars will disappear
But wherever the road takes you on your travels
Once you've settled down, you'll realise
You've never really left here

# DIRTY BARS

*Shout out to Dirty Bars, when I first heard your lyrics,*
*I was in awe. Thank you for paving the way.*

That's the way I'm flowing
Always moving
Always growing
Never slowing down

I wanna be that boy who's big from ill-town
I'm underground
Want to break through to the overground
This is serious sh*t
Bars I ain't playing around.

# ᴵLFORD ᴮOYS

Catch the Overground, with no joy
You will fall in love with an Ilford boy
He's got you a Rubicon mango and packet of chilli
  McCoy's
It is what it is, so you need to find a way to enjoy

He's got ambitious dreams
Side-parting hair
He'll take you to Valentines Park, in the huts by
  the cafe,
All the masterminds are there

He's underachieving in school
Brilliant at swinging back on the chair
You better be good at running on the buses
Around here, they're always hopping the fares

They love their movies that are for over-15s
The daytime raves for under-16s
They lose every football match
But convinced that they have such a sick team
If you don't know what he's saying
Ultimately you will know what he means

If you're still with him once he's left school
  It's a life of chicken shops and barbers
Road man and charmers
Mixed religious couples
Tensions and dramas
Potentially be at sixth forms with the clever kids
Who act like the bad things they never did
Never inherited knowledge, wealth or privilege

But the most beautiful thing is that their audacity is
  absolutely everything

PS Good luck with an Ilford Boy.

# ALL I NEED

I'm a slow guy with a smartphone
Who still spills food on his top
Whilst constantly fighting with the stone in my sock
I'm hiding from Debenhams staff whilst spraying on
   tester Hugo Boss,
I live at home with my damp-fighting wallpaper and my
   half-decent laptop,
And you know what?
It's all I need
I hang over the staircase and scream
'Mum, what's for dinner?'
Please,
If I'm not asking Siri I'm asking Jeeves,
I love staring at photos of sunsets and trees
And it's all I need
I don't care for music that's the latest
I'm stuck for life with my nineties R&B playlist
Overdrawn, maxed out, bank balance payments
But I still sing in the shower
Like I'm the greatest
I tried a cigarette once
I started choking
I always leave the bathroom floor soaking
I'm that one friend who takes banter way too far and
   then I'm like, 'Ah chill out, I'm joking'
Some people say I got a small lisp
Tell you the truth
My petrol light's always on
I take midnight strolls to the fridge
And stare into it like that's where I belong
My iPhone wire requires a delicate hand
I've figured out the method - I can give you the cheat

You hold it like
And you turn it like that
And hopefully your phone charges
But being 26, the biggest achievement was figuring out
  how to successfully change my bed sheets
I'm forever trying to lose weight
Then debating my hair line is fading
'Excuse me, I'd like more food on my plate'
I say I'm patient but I hate waiting
I love to laugh so much it hurts
I say I'm full but I've always got room for dessert
And the craziest thing of all
In my life, I spent countless hours
Being stuck on the Underground
With one headphone that works
I've realised having a degree really doesn't mean nothing
My teeth, on the other hand, always need more brushing
I enjoy long walks and more hugging
And I tell my friends I'm outside when really I'm still
  en route coming
And it's all I need
A smile from my best mate's bent teeth
Conversations that go well deep,
Walks in the park so I can breathe is all I need
I'm learning to take life for what it is
To give more
Argue less and forever dream
To walk on air and fly through clouds
Is all I need
And yeah, I'm always pretending to not be too mainstream
And my elbows are dry, I still need to cream
Me and the boys have the worst five-a-side football team
But it's all I want

      Because truthfully it's all I need.

# THE ARTISTIC COMMUNITY

*In order for your dreams to have the best chance of
thriving and surviving, you must implement a sustainable
business model to run alongside them x*

I represent all my singers that are working in retail
Where you hang up your harmonies and vocals and pay more
    attention to customer detail

I speak for all my actors who stand in bars pouring drinks
Who work through the night to pay rent
The only rest you have is when your eyes blink

I shake a leg for my dancers
Who spend their lives in auditions
Where you sacrifice your diet and fitness - all for that
    perfect precision

I nod my head for my bedroom producers
Where keyboards meet logic
And you've created history with your computers, all to
    be taken for masses by the consumers

I hold my hands up for my poets and authors
Who have kept the book alive in an age of e-torture

And I salute all my creatives who are responsible for
    innovation
But go unnoticed, because they do it for the love, and
    not a standing ovation

I feel the pain in my fellow extras
Who wake up early to be on set

Forgetting how many times you missed breakfast
Just hoping your TV time is more than a sec

I look at billboards twice for my graphic designers
Who create legacies with mice and track pads,
And tell us a thousand stories through visual effects –
  you image writers

I step aside for my runners on set
Who share the vision of the directors, but for now will
  be responsible for fetching a bottle of water and a
  baguette
Your time is coming; just hold on a sec

You always hear that, and you always hear this
If you're waiting for a sign in life, hand on my heart
  this is it
My artistic community, believe me it's worth the risk.

# CHANGING THE NARRATIVE

Rapunzel, Rapunzel you can cut your hair,
As I am no longer walking up walls,
As from tonight I am climbing up stairs

Humpty, Humpty please come down from that wall,
From this moment you will stand, and stand you will tall,

When you walk through these corridors you make way for
  Hagrid
And when you walk through the shire you shake hands with
  Mr Baggins

Aslan, I first heard you roar,
The moment I pressed through my closet door

Fiona, pack your bags and say farewell to this swamp
Because you have clicked your heels for far too long
  down this yellow brick road and tonight you will stop

Pinocchio, please realise it will shrink gradually
Elphaba take his hand, as you both will now defy gravity

And Aladdin, don't you dare not invite Jasmine too
For the final performance of *The Taming of the Shrew*

Jack inform Jill she no longer needs to repent
As I too take tribute, so let these Hunger Games commence

Cinderella, your sisters will have to obey
As we have now discovered 50 more shades to that dark,
  dismal grey

Simba do not weep, as you're soon to be king
As it spreads through the land, the valleys, the
  meadows, I hear the bluebirds sing
And let's ring these bells of Notre Dame,
As Snow White has been captured by 14 little arms

Dumbo, when you fly, make sure you never land,
You wave to Alice when you gracefully pass through her
  wonderland

So the boy never grew up,
Peter's theory was correct
And he lives inside all of us,
Therefore this story reconnects

And as this fairy tale continues
And this saga goes on
You start to realise your happily ever after
Was never far gone
Because good overcomes evil,
Your legend will always triumph
Which is why I look to the sky every time I hear the
  name David
But make acceptance to understand Goliath

So if this once upon a time,
Was genuinely once upon a time

Time converts it to money, which makes it once upon a
  dime
And life in itself makes it once upon a climb
So here on onwards makes it once upon a crime
To hear what you've heard and not think
Once upon a sign

From Jumanji to Madagascar
Narnia through to Caspar
Ramallah to Alaska
Everything you read adds to your chapter

Now I can smile, not knowing the answer
And conclude my story with eventually, they all lived
   happily ever after.

# I Stole My Mother's Jewellery

From as early as I could remember, she would wear it
  without fail
Through nocturnal periods, we would watch as it would
  set sail
As it floats through this moonlit sky, in abundance it
  takes flight
This was not your ordinary fairy tale

For I stole my mother's jewellery,
In the room when it was pitch black
For I stole my mother's jewellery
And I am never giving it back

They say a diamond is a woman's best friend
Within these words I delve and I fail to comprehend
As carved as this ruby lies,
Engraved with her final touch
I begin to commend,
For I know,
All will be mine in the end

For these pearls that I have lifted
Create the fruits of my soul
As a thief of the trimester I wonder,
As I swim my final stroll

For the most sacred jewel of all,
Is the stone that is deemed forbidden
But she gave it to me, she gave it,
Therefore her jewellery was never hidden

For I stole my mother's jewellery,
In the room when it was pitch black
For I stole my mother's jewellery
And I am never giving it back

For the smiles these stones have risen
This jewellery she had never bought
This crime of theft leads not to prison
Instead to an abundance of lessons I was taught

Behold an inheritance of extreme measure
The finest wisdom beyond its years
Weighing in carats and gold this hidden treasure
For what's mine is yours, she said, my dear

Whatever sparkles my child on earth
You are to share it with whoever
For you are soon to realise on new birth
That your diamonds will live forever

So did I steal my mother's jewellery?
With elegance and slight charm
As I smashed through her bedroom window
Without raising the home alarm,

For I am a citizen who is law-abiding
This court hearing lasted longer than expected
I am wearing all of her jewellery with none in hiding
It may not have been what you expected

Did I steal my mother's jewellery,
  In the room when it was pitch black?
And if I stole my mother's jewellery,

Tell me,

How could I ever give it back?

# FRIDAY NIGHT

Friday night at my desktop
Lost in rhyme with no fresh crop
Where's my mind - gone - when I reflect on
The city nights of my younger life now I got no effect on

My mood when it needs stabilising
Always been true, never plagiarising
Lost the solitude when the boat started capsizing
Politics is rude, only good for gaslighting

A temperament that's overthinking
Every elephant and element I'm down 'n sinking
It's hard to sleep when the settlement's interlinking
Your skeleton is now hurt when your soul is shrinking

Forget all of this, day ones I'm linking.

# DEAR OLD HUSSAIN

I miss the warmth,
The kindness of your heart
Your rubbish jokes
Your slow driving
Your incapability to fake laugh
Dear old Hussain,
We went from bubble baths to thinking we're psychopaths

These demons came in
They took over your planet
They flipped the script
Took the mick
And it's very hard to imagine

The days we had no stress
We had life on balance
But Hussain I really need you right now
Too much has happened

We need to find a cure
I know we can find it
I am 100 per cent sure
So when you do, don't hide it

We can rebuild our kingdom
As if we are kings and queens
Princes and princesses
Like when we were kids with dreams
Be there for you
Before you can be there for me
That doesn't make you selfish
Get over yourself

Because there is a world that needs your help quick

And until the next time we meet
I hope you're still singing our tune
Remember, out of the darkest nights shine the most
  powerful of moons
They might leave you with scars
But I hope through all this time
You have learnt to be proud of your battle wounds

I hope to never see you again soon.

## Chapter Two

# My Problem Is I Care Too Much

I never really planned to become an 'activist', and even saying that word now makes me really question and wonder whether I am one. Speaking up on issues was just something I found I started doing when I was feeling things in my heart that would cause me emotional distress and would stop me from sleeping. There are many times in my life when I have found I am moving out of how I am feeling. When I first heard in the early 2000s that there was flooding in Pakistan, I organised a fundraising dinner and took 16 of the boys I grew up with to climb Ben Nevis in Fort William, Scotland to raise awareness and funds to help people rebuild their homes.

Shortly after this, another mountain climb was on the cards and this time it was to help the people of Palestine who desperately needed aid. We took a trip to Snowdonia in Wales and this time the group was much larger. I felt these fundraising efforts were essential things I had to do, but I also felt as though they were a responsibility.

I went on to spend 19 days in Gaborone, Botswana helping rebuild a small village with worn-out car tyres that we'd fill with sand to create cement and pile on top of each other. After Botswana, I found myself on Mount Kilimanjaro, again raising awareness for the Pakistan flood victims as, by this point, 20 million people had been displaced.

I spent a vast amount of time travelling across the United States meeting people who had suffered tragic injustice, shootings, brutality and so much more. All of this fuelled my passion to do something to help, and make the world a better place. I also undertook various trips to numerous refugee camps across Europe to help provide aid, shelter and some form of hope to those fleeing war-torn countries for a better life.

I once left my home after watching a video online of a young Syrian refugee boy named Mohammed Abdelmajeed, aged seven at the time. He spoke of his rare connective tissue genetic disorder and all he asked for was a friend to tell him he was handsome. I packed a bag and headed to Athens in Greece as rumour had it that he was there at the time. I met my good friend Imran there and together we went through the camps in search of this young man. From there, we went to more camps in Thessaloniki and the search continued. It was cold, it was snowing, it was freezing, and many people in these camps were becoming very ill due to the severe conditions.

However, we didn't stop. We heard from a non-government organisation that Mohammed was in Turkey. Imran took me to the airport and I did what I needed to do – I boarded a plane to a country I had never been to before and searched the camps of Istanbul, but still found no signs of this young man. All of this time I had no intention of showing the world what I was doing; I just wanted to travel to him and tell him, 'You are very handsome.' I carried on going – the search was tough; I didn't speak the languages of the spaces and places I was entering, but when I have a goal in mind I will not stop until I reach it. At this point, the producer of the original video messaged me as word had got round at the camps and he told me he could take me to meet Mohammed, but I was in the wrong place. I needed to go to a place called Batman, also in Turkey. I boarded another plane and landed in Batman.

It was here that I met with the producer, from another non-government organisation, and together we formulated a plan. I asked what essential things the family needed right now and he said money for rent,

clothes and toys for the children as they were living
in exceptionally tough and very rough conditions. We
went to a supermarket and I purchased all the toys and
clothes I could carry. I then asked if it would be
suitable for me to ask the people who follow my work
online to help this cause and everyone agreed. We went
live on the internet and donations poured in. We also
created a video, which went on to receive millions of
views, and the world became further aware of Mohammed
and his condition.

I stepped back at this point - it had become way
bigger than me - but I was just glad that I had been
able to play a small role in helping this story gain
the awareness it needed in a respectable manner. And the
most beautiful part of it all was watching Mohammed's
smile grow into a cheeky laugh the moment my words were
translated into his language and he heard how handsome I
think he is.

This was something I will cherish forever.

Prior to meeting Mohammed and attempting to help
him, a significant moment in my life happened that
contributed very heavily to the man, writer, poet and
'activist' I am today: I won a trip to space at the
One Young World Summit. I won this trip after beating
thousands of contestants from all across the world
through the Rising Star competition. I had no intention
of going into space to begin with and this was heavily
documented throughout my entire process as I was more
interested in being able to utilise a platform on a
global scale to hopefully influence and create some form
of change in the way the world treats and discusses mental
health and those suffering in silence with the illness.

I remember very clearly, I performed 'My Name
Is Hussain' to three of my close friends at Jasmine

Jethwa's house in Ilford. That moment was really key;
I thank those three immensely for that night. It's
November 2015 and the world is still not speaking
about mental health issues, so just before I headed to
Bangkok, Thailand to participate in the summit's final,
my close 'day one' friendship circle and I went to
Nandos, Beckton for a farewell/good luck meal.

When we got to the car park to say goodbye, I asked
my friends if they wanted to hear my speech. They all
stood around my Toyota Yaris and I wound down the
windows, played Hans Zimmer music from YouTube and
performed my heart out. I still remember this moment
like it was yesterday, even though it was more than five
years ago now, and I recall how thrilled and excited my
friends were (which is rare for my day one friendship
group - I am normally greeted with a barrage of 'You can
do better!').

Anyway, back to Thailand and the summit! The late
Kofi Annan, Bob Geldof, Fatima Bhutto, astronaut
Ron Garan, and so many more world leaders were in
attendance. My name was called and I took to the stage
- I had three minutes to deliver a speech of a lifetime.
Little did I know that performance was to change my life
forever. A very special mention to Emma for all you did
throughout this entire process, and beyond. I hope when
you have this book in your hands and you are reading it
you are smiling knowing that your boy never gave up and
he kept pushing through! And of course Stephen, my man,
and all the team involved in my life during that period.
You were crucial in helping me become who I am today.

Not only did I win a trip to space, I left Thailand
with the courage to come back and partner with King's
College London and Hackney Empire to set the Guinness
World Record for the 'world's largest mental health

lesson' educating the most young people simultaneously on subjects such as depression, anxiety, self-harm, stigma and taboo. It was truly iconic. I must mention Yamin, you are a very special man. Thank you for allowing me the platform, the opportunity and the chance to come to Hackney Empire to deliver this. Your belief in me has always pushed me, you have helped so many of us and I need you to know how much love I have for you my brother. Like we always say, 'we are only just getting started'.

To tell you the truth, I still don't know if I am an activist; I just like to do things when my heart tells me they need to be done and this was a significant chapter in my life. 'My Name Is Hussain' was the piece that changed my life, but during that period there was so much more poetry that the world never saw, heard or felt. It was written to help me process, understand and make sense of the things I was witnessing.

Enough of me keeping them to myself; it's time I shared them. Thanks for still being with me on this journey. We're doing great - we've reached Chapter Two! And it is called ...

My Problem Is I Care Too Much.

# MY NAME IS HUSSAIN

Hello, my name is Hussain
And my problem is I care too much
And the following may leave your mind state in a twirl
Therefore, ladies and gentleman, I apologise for the
  inconvenience, but I'm trying to change the world


Dear Mum,
I wasn't meant for this planet
You did everything you could, so please don't panic
No one likes me so I might as well vanish


I wear jumpers to hide the stories I write on my arm
Only I can read them, but the doctor calls it 'self-
  harm'.
If I bleed they tell me to put on a plaster
But if I'm depressed inside there is no bandage for this
  internal disaster


But it's all right Mum, I found a cure
I'm no longer alone
The callings come
You see, God's me calling me home


What about the soldiers Mum?
The torment of the mind,
The flashbacks of deaths, the sounds of innocent cries
Do we expect them to have a healthy state of mind?
Negative soldier, good job but access denied


My sisters I'm with you until the end
Over 100 million who are currently living with the
  consequences of FGM

Female mutilation, to me that's physiological poverty
The inhumane degrading treatment of gender inequality

Stranded boats, high waves,
Abandoned homes, lack of aid
My refugees, I feel the pain
The sanctuary of your minds is something we need to save

When I say 'Mum', I mean Mother Nature
She created us all so together we should be greater
But mentally where we stand I am not in favour
And to me that problem, couldn't be any greater

Am I going too deep?
Is this enough?
Two pence in a McDonald's box, a dollar in a homeless
  man's cup,
Thinking I can't do no more but give two pounds a month
Well, there is one thing more,
And that thing is love
Some love too much, and are in love with themselves
Whilst others don't love at all, and the problem is
  themselves

Hello, my name is Hussain and my problem is I care
  too much

We can put a man on the moon
We can discover life on Mars
But we can't give our children food

Mentally we have become detached from ourselves and society
Tell me it's OK not to be OK, but don't tell me quietly
One rising star alone cannot light up this sky

Which is why I'm here to create an army of fireflies
To spread love through towns, cities and deep within
　　tribes
Only then will this one young world learn how to survive

Give me a chance to go to space to look down on the
　　world's land and see
Then I can land and see
Where to plant my rising star seed
But for now I'll use the sky as our commonality
From the Amazon, to high-rises to out of this galaxy
Mental health matters
And that's the reality

And as you can probably tell, I care too much
And the previous may have left your mind state in a twirl
Therefore, ladies and gentleman, I apologise for the
　　inconvenience, but I'm going to change the world.

# THE FLARE

I'm ready to shoot my flare in the sky
Injustice is willing for us to die
And our wings aren't helping us fly
I'm ready to shoot my flare in the sky

This is for the justice,
This is for the writers,
This is for the pain,
This is for the lighters,
This one's for my mind,
This is for my fighters,
And this one's in your feelings
Because this one's for my riders

I'm speaking for the famine
I'm writing for the pilgrims
I use my voice for my sisters
I scream and shake my words for my children
I feel the pain of innocent single dads, who mentally
  never made it back
Life can present real invisible oppression
I'm not here to entertain any surface-level chitter-chat

Little man's, getting stopped, on his block,
Because of the shine on his watch,
By a uniformed bad man,
A real crooked cop,
If you zoom out,
We look like we're the ones
Who lost the plot,
Because there's not much we got
But a step and a bop

Disoriented, we're lost
In the game versus the boss
It's time we untie the knots,
And go shoot the shot
If we don't then we lost
All the little we got
Let me meet you at the drop
I'll get the game on lock
Once and for all,
We can finally get on top


Because if you answer back, believe it or not, then we
  fail
The only sentence you know, will be the one that's in jail
There's no chance to prevail
Or set sail, my brother, just breathe, but don't be too
  angry when you exhale
They look for the smallest reason in your detail
The most minor of your movements against injustice
Have the largest effect on the most major of scale
Many of us never could relate to the books we read
  growing up
Because when you're living in a nightmare,
It's a mockery; they present you with fiction and fairy
  tales
My brother, relax, breathe, inhale,
Don't let their bias, prejudice, discrimination
Be the reason your train derails
But he reacted, his anger full-scale
He didn't,
We failed


I'm ready to shoot my flare in the sky
Too many of us are daring to die

And our wings aren't helping us fly
I'm ready to shoot my flare in the sky


Mum's waiting up for her son to come home
Dad's on night shift, don't know that the problem's his
  own
Little man's lost in the streets, a phone full of
  numbers
But not one he can phone
Another shot bagged, another vision there zoned,
Sister's waiting by her window at night
Waiting to sneak her brother in right,
She sits and she's tired,
Then can't wake up for school
Her mum thinks she's being disobedient
Punishes her for breaking the rules
They don't understand,
She took one for the team
Her brother's ungrateful
Shows no respect as it seems
She carries on doing it,
Knows she's his lifeline and her role is vital
Because if she don't let him in,
He won't ever come back
And she knows her little brother from that point will be
Forever lost in the streets, cycle,

She knows too well, if presented to court,
A judge will take one look, and the sentence will be
  harsh
She studies media, sociology and psychology and
  understands if he goes down
Sympathy is not a question
No one will march

Society's branded Pakistanis as terrorists, and other
  things dark
She can't speak to her brother; he's not down to
  question
A self-fulfilling catastrophe, with no one to listen
So she studies to be a lawyer,
Her books catch the tears from her eyes
And when the hammer bangs,
She goes into her room and prepares to shoot her flare
  in the sky

Because Injustice is willing for us to die
And our wings aren't helping us fly
I'm ready to shoot my flare in the sky

Injustice has overstayed its welcome
It's something we have to terminate
We can't allow it to alienate, duplicate, dominate,
Definitely causing us further psychological anxiety
We can't allow our pride to segregate
Tearing us further apart
Whilst it discriminates and eliminates a chance for us
  to activate
Mental freedom of our psychiatry
We gather and won't do it quietly
For those on the sentence it's a heavy weight
Which is why we must advocate
And we can't do that silently

I'm ready to shoot my flare in the sky
Injustice is willing for us to die
And our wings aren't helping us fly
I'm ready to shoot my flare in the sky

# LIFE IS SAD & BEAUTIFUL

This is for the justice,
This is for the writers,
This is for the pain,
This is for the lighters,
This one's for my mind,
This is for my fighters,
And this one's in your feelings
Because this one's for my riders

I'm speaking for the famine
I'm writing for the pilgrims
I use my voice for my sisters
I shout for my children
I feel the pain of innocent single dads, who mentally
  never made it back
Life can present real invisible oppression
I'm not here to entertain any surface-level chat.

# HABIBA AND HAROON

They met online
She swiped right
He started to type
And before you know it, they met for a bite
It was good conversations, nothing to put on the
internet for likes
It was private, it felt right
Their connection grew, and before you knew it time did fly

She said I want you to meet my family
He said yeah of course,
None of him felt anxiously
Haroon treated Habiba like a queen,
She was his majesty
In her friendship groups they're already talking wedding
décor, dresses, starters, and canapes
His boys are talking stags, Dubai, Vegas, Morocco,
everyone's moving happily

She runs down the stairs, and says
Mum, we need to clean the room, he will be here soon,
Hoping and praying it goes smooth,
Haroon had a shape up, not too flashy but smelt of
Chanel blue,
Well groomed, on arrival through the front door he met
Ali,
Habiba's little brother, and the stars aligned them two
got along too
Now everyone's amused, it's real it's genuine with not
too much to prove
Everyone approved

They walked him to the door, she walked him to the car,
Starring into each other's eyes,
and that's when he said, ok I met your parents,
I think it's time you and your family came and met mine,

Different villages from back home
But nobody seemed to care
Samosa, pakora flying everywhere,
Talks of venues, DJ's, dates, dholkhi nights, it's an
incredible atmosphere

Habiba and Haroon are getting engaged
Get the marquee up, the lights on the house,
Let's build the stage, together they are starting to
write a new page

The mehndi nights of singing
Two families coming together, dancing and grinning
Everyone winning, thanking the lord, everyone living

It's time for the wedding
Everyone's invited
Ali got a rental, to drive his sister to the hall
He's overly excited,
both parents and families are delighted
a love ignited
and they pray together both of them stay guided

Camera man's filming people eating food
Random aunties and uncles coming on the stage for photos
skipping the queue
Habiba doesn't care
Neither does Haroon
They've waited for a companionship like this and soon

They'll be living happily ever after
In their own place
With no in-law drama

The DJ said it's the final song
Habiba looks at her mother and father
Realising this is it,
Scarf over her head to cover her trembling lip
Daddies' little princess
Is about to start a new journey in her life
With a new flame that's been lit

She walks out of the hall slowly
Beji and Baba are praying for a life to be well and holy

She gets outside
Haroon's by the car
She waves to her family and grabs Ali by his arm,
She says take care of mum and dad, I won't be far

They close the door
The car begins to start
They chase it out the venue
And off she's gone with all of her family in her heart

The party's over
Everyone's leaving
Ali and his boys got the rental
So to them the city they are scheming
A night worth exploring and dreaming

He tells his dad, I'm going out with the boy's I'll be
back late in the evening

And his dad says, ok beta, drive safe

Without any meaning
The windows down, roof off,
Headlights beaming

Habiba's with Haroon,
Overwhelmed controlling her breathing
Emotional but believing

Her mother's back at home finding things to be cleaning
Her father's drinking tea, talking to his brothers about
life and its meaning

And then the phone rings
The mother screams with what the news brings
They all look in disbelief
They can't believe
The news they just received

Habiba's taking off her make up,
Haroon's hanging up his clothes
She answers her phone and can't believe the tone

Back at home, their mother's screaming it's mental
Haroon looks at Habiba and says what happened

Ali and his friends lost control of the car,
They died, he died inside of a rental

You Are

*Invited*

To The Walima of

Habiba & Haroon

# No More Lonely

Loneliness, I mean I've felt it
Honestly speaking, I won't lie, I have too,
I learnt what I began feeling mentally, eventually,
  impacted me physically
I'm so glad we're speaking about this because it's true
Through the effects of the pandemic
And everything else we have all individually,
  collectively been through
Many of us have felt lonely and that we can't let
  continue
So, let's use today to reach out to each other, through
  the isolation
To build on our relations,
Using empathy, time, and care to develop consideration
For every single one of us from every generation
To feel and be connected to reach you via the radio in
  your location
Together we can overcome loneliness
To aid our mental well-being and we start this
Through the powerful art of communication
Using the real-life conversation

# I'M ASHAMED

I'm ashamed to be a citizen of this world
Where we breed corruption, deceit and inequality between
  boys and girls
I'm ashamed of myself
Indulged in temptation, desire and wealth
I'm so ashamed I don't cry, I laugh

I'm ashamed my grandparents fought for my education
  whilst I bunked in the park
I'm ashamed at my work rate, the generation before us
  kept it together and worked hard
I'm ashamed we let the smallest things get
Political and tear us apart

I'm ashamed we value success via likes and shares
I'm ashamed we spend our pay cheques dancing to techno
  sounds, drums and snares
House parties, raves, West End bottles and flares
I'm so ashamed that I don't even care

I'm ashamed we are so connected and equally disconnected
  simultaneously
I'm ashamed we watch polar ice caps melt and think it's
  happened spontaneously

I'm ashamed that when I look up to the sky and think of
  my contribution
It's half-hearted prayers from my attic window and bags
  full of pollution

I'm ashamed my footprint is made of carbon
I'm ashamed I find more peace and solace with E. K.
  watching *In the Night Garden*
I'm ashamed I burden my friendships with A. K. and S. P.
And then send messages in the morning saying sorry about
  that, it's cool now
I can manage

I'm ashamed we are looked at by colour
I'm ashamed our phones connect quicker to the internet
  in someone's home then our hearts do with each other

I'm ashamed the media has become a weapon of mass
  distraction
I'm ashamed the world is great at causing further divide
  and subtraction

I'm ashamed that the people of Rohingya are facing
  injustice within our eyes
I'm ashamed to be alive in a time where we are still
  using words like 'holocaust' and 'genocide'
I'm ashamed it's even a debate that Sandra Bland
  committed suicide

I'm ashamed freedom doesn't come freely
I'm ashamed we don't know the name or the whole story of
  Aafia Siddiqui

I'm ashamed that in my throat I feel a lump
And ashamed till the death of me that hundreds of years
  of slavery is only taught in a single month

I'm ashamed we did the mannequin challenge whilst the
  orphans were calling

I'm ashamed that Syria has lost its children and Aleppo
   has fallen
I'm ashamed we didn't focus in history and ran through
   our corridors
When we should have been learning about Kunta Kinte, Anne
   Frank and how much heart it took to escape from Sobibor

I'm ashamed our intelligence is artificial and cannot
   breathe
I'm ashamed we created a virtual world because we
   destroyed the world we can really see:
I'm ashamed we elected world leaders that cannot lead

I'm ashamed terror has depressed the planet
I'm ashamed anxiety is imbedding itself in the granite

I'm ashamed we will take this moment for what it is
And in a few hours be even more ashamed because I'll
   continue like it didn't exist

We travelled fast
But we moved slow,
We developed quick,
We didn't grow

I learnt it all on Wanstead Park Bridge,
In Valentines Park and Belgrave Road
One thing I'm not ashamed to say is this is home
   sweet home.

# ᴜɴᴅᴇʀ ᴛʜᴇ ᴄᴀʀᴘᴇᴛ

All divorce talk goes under the carpet
Mental health - under the carpet
Drugs and issues, guess what it knows?
That it goes under the carpet
Politics, under the carpet
Truth about world peace? Under the carpet
So I know it always looks nice, but the real question
  is, what's under the carpet?

Family drama, under the carpet
Thoughts and feelings, under the carpet
And that little thing that you bought at the market
  speaks a lot of pain because it matches the carpet

Oh what?
You're a rapper now? No, but the boy had to chance it
Now I'm in the right lane, so I might blast it
I came from the waves on the back of a hardship

All divorce talk goes under the carpet
Mental health - under the carpet
Drugs and issues, guess what it knows?
That it goes under the carpet
Politics, under the carpet
Truth about world peace? Under the carpet
So I know it always looks nice, but the real question
  is, what's under the carpet?

I learnt from Jay-Z and J. Cole to look under the carpet
And the real ones are there, and they'll carry the
  burden and halve it
The love's too real when you don't have to ask it

They'll help you face every little thing that's under
  the carpet
And I need to answer
If a boy like me has come from the dark, yet,
Because Mum's not here and I know if she was, she'd ask it

Many nights I woke up panicking
But I came through battling
I came from the jungle where the snakes put the rattles in
Microphone's splattering, it wasn't COD battering
But that's not the problem
When energy's what's the matter in

I'm an empath
I kind of feel too much
But, you know me, and when I say I'm too tough
But the world needs one thing and that's love, because
  where I come from we don't give too much

Domestic violence?
Under the carpet
Racist families?
Under the carpet
Cheating partners live under the carpet
It's not just floorboards that are under your carpet
Hidden agendas
Under the carpet
Skeletons straight from the casket
And every little thing that's in there from you, yes,
  you guessed it, it's under the carpet.

We ain't got a clue what's behind closed doors,
We ain't got a clue what's behind those floors
And the truth of the matter is that when you put it on

the platter,
The government holds off chords
It hits real hard when you deep it,
Because we all feel it but won't speak it
And we're just looking at our kids and we're scared deep
    down that we might teach it.

But when something's under the carpet,
You don't talk about it.
You bleep it.
There's no matter with the fact because at that point
    you accept it that you can't cheat it.
And the Lord knows you tried to beat it.
But don't give up. You don't need it.
Do you remember how good it felt to be you? When?
    Remember, you been it.

So Grandma's love, you put under the carpet.
Happiness, you put under the carpet.
Imagine everything you'd find if you went and looked
    right under the carpet.

Memories, under the carpet
Sibling love was under the carpet
Every conversation that needed to be had - had under the
    carpet
Grief and loss, under the carpet
Depression's a boss under the carpet
You just go in and ask why are you lot all under the carpet?

Gender equality, under the carpet
The refugees that conversation can't stay, under the carpet
Police brutality, guess what it knows? That it goes
    under the carpet.

# YOUR VOICE

I don't know you
But this is for you, we owe you
Your voice spoke for my closest half
For that I wish, we wish, we could hold you
To thank you
For you to feel our warmth
As there would have been times you would have felt the
    cold too


But, look,
We don't know you
But we thank you
And very high we hold you
Your voice
Your words
Set peace
Set terms
Calmed many of our griefs
Calmed many of our nerves
Thank you for giving us what he deserves


But, look,
We don't know you
But we thank you
And whoever you are, wherever you are,
Just know it's very high
Where we hold you
Your voice spoke for my closest half
For that I wish, we wish, we could hold you
To thank you
For you to feel our warmth
As there would have been times you would have felt the
    cold too.

# BELGRAVE ROAD

I'm just sitting here talking to Dad about
  gentrification
We've reached past the set of problems that were skilled
  enough for our parents to go into their investigations
Here's a compilation
Life will take parts of you
This is real-life operation
Of the pain of my generation


And when people look at me and say, 'What's he going
  to start?'


Tell them I said, 'A conversation'


Gather around; I need you lot to witness this
They want to say the women of my culture are oppressed
I'm not sure what they think this is
Not realising how many of our women are running their
  own businesses
Planting things from the ground up
Feeding the family, capturing images of the food
Redefining photosynthesis
Not sure what many of you think this is.

# Know Your Rights

My brothers on road, know your rights
My sisters at home, know your rights
The girls in the hood, know your rights
The boys in the books, know your rights
When you step outside, know your rights
For a stop and search, know your rights

There's another way you can put up a fight
It's really round one, when you know your rights

First things first, there's manipulation
When they analyse your situation
Even if you're filming it
For certain coppers there's no hesitation
It's you versus them in the conversation
They don't lose there's a compilation
They get to keep their job there's a combination
On top of that they get compensation

The law enforcement, the justice system
What do you think? For us it's written?
It's all lies, their figures are hidden
All child's play, they say that 'they didn't'

The way we're getting treated is not all right
In the courtroom we are losing the fight
On the side of the road we are losing our lives
From the off we don't know our rights

My brothers on road, know your rights
My sisters at home, know your rights
The girls in the hood, know your rights

The boys in the books, know your rights
When you step outside, know your rights
For a stop and search, know your rights

There's another way you can put up a fight
It's really round one, when you know your rights

When you're trapped in your life by a system
We have to praise the ones who broke through, who have
   risen
When we talk mental health, we must speak for the ones
   in prison
Where PTSD is something you adopt
Depression is something many have got
Rehabilitation is a long shot
It's like trying to find a clean heart in a dirty cop

My brothers on road, I need you to know your rights
My sisters at home, I need you to know your rights
The girls in the hood, I need you to know your rights
The boys in the books, I need you to know your rights
When you step outside, I need you to know your rights
For a stop and search, I need you to know your rights

Little old me, telling a tale
Too many of us stood in the eyes of the law
And the system always failed
From that, I had enough dark nights, praying Christian
   made bail

Here's what I want, an explanation
Before you begin my investigation
Name and constable's number
So we can all get down in this situation

Here's something you are meant to tell me
I don't need to give no information
Unless I give you an invitation
I just need to give a brief explanation

Here's what I want
A same-sex officer
You're on my time
So hurry up officer
And I'm going to film it
Because I can
And you're going to say
No one's stopping ya
Detain me?
On what grounds?
Discrimination?
Na, not now!
Look, you can stop now
Don't make me show you what my brain's got now

Stereotypes, I got rights
False accusations, I got rights
For injustice, I got rights
And everything right now, is not right
On the side of the road, I won't fight
That's what they want, on site
But I am telling you now, it's not right

I need you to know your rights.

# THE ANIMAL KINGDOM

On behalf of the human race
This is a letter
One I felt very guilty and ashamed to write
And it is addressed to the animal kingdom

I'm sorry we failed you
All of us had a part to play
I have to admit it
We pretty much nailed you

We saw your homes get smaller and smaller
And then we hung you in cages in our offices and homes
Glamorising the fact that we jailed you
Oh, the animal kingdom
How we failed you

How us human beings hunt you for nothing but glory
You really don't deserve to live in history just yet
There's so much more for you to do to live out your story
I had to write this
For you, for me
I just feel as guilty for doing nothing
And I can't do nothing
I must do something
Because you gave me something
You gave me a feeling when you saw me

That's to giraffes
I can't believe I'm saying this, but I will miss you
How your structure built so magnificent
In today's world should be far from extinct
I can't believe we silently allowed people to kill you

# MY PROBLEM IS I CARE TOO MUCH

To the tigers
I can't believe we built machines to outskill you
To trip you up and drill you
I can't believe we've let it come to this
There are millions of us that feel you

To the gorillas
The King Kongs
I don't know if you know
You are the hero in our movies
I still can't believe we got you wrong
The way you slam your feet
And we see ashes rise of sediment
How your silhouette against the sunset and sunrise moves
  and glides so elegant
The way your horn stretches far looks dangerously
  delicate
How your tusk shoots water so eloquent
I'm sad to say I will be alive during the time extinct
  was the elephant

We can't let them die and only be alive to live in fiction
We can't let them be left with the dirty hands of hunters
We can't as humans cause them friction

Let their language be one where we sit in silence,
  respect, appreciate and listen

The animal kingdom
Is one of the greatest gifts earth was ever given.

# I AM KAAVAN

*Mum - our efforts to save Kaavan really helped. You was
the only woman in the room with the zookeepers, the
mahouts and associates, some of whom were armed. I couldn't
have been more proud and scared for us. Kaavan is now
free and in the wild. I thought you might like to know.*

I am Sri Lankan born
Dark-skinned
Equipped with my mother's touch
My father's wings

I am a national treasure
A childhood dream
A standing story
A lifelong scene

I am perseverance
I am determination
I am patience and tolerance
I am freedom, and not just freedom in the imagination

I am the people that gave their heart
For all animals in captivity who silently scream
I am Kaavan
I am free.

# THE SCIENTIST

Broken stairs
Creaking floorboards
Damp-fighting wallpaper
Human warlords
Torn bed sheets
Unlocking doors
Flickering light bulbs
Cement-paved floors
Gentle fingers
Vigorous hands
No visa requirements
On my tourist land
Length of stay
Long-haul, some minimal
Holy waters
Far from biblical
It's so easy to gain access to a passage
To enter with a hefty package
And leave the room damaged
With cold, wet baggage
Currency savage
Is this the new classic?
Strangle my throat until I can no longer breathe
My eyelids water, my shaking rattled teeth
For a bank note I will barely ever see
Dare to think, what lies beneath

A distraught specimen
There's multicultural evidence
No set medicine
For this bed-bound veteran
Whose eyes are no longer genuine

Leaves a testament
They walk as gentlemen
For their returning resident
Inside of them she placed a sentiment
An explosive elephant
Embedded in their skeleton
I think it's excellent
Of course, this was your laboratory
But it was her experiment.

# THE REGISTER

Teacher: Kyle
Student: Yes sir

Teacher: Ethan
Student: Yes sir

Teacher: Brenton
Student: Yes sir

Teacher: Aafia
*Silence*

Teacher: Is Aafia here?
Student: No sir

Teacher: Where is she?
Student: She's at the FMC Carswell Prison in Fort Worth
  Texas

Teacher: OK, right, let's not talk about this

Teacher: Jeffrey?
Student: Yes sir.

# SUPERHEROES NEEDED: APPLY HERE

This, is a superhero calling,
We as humanity, have dropped the ball,
But yet, we believe, we're balling,
We've lost our drive as humans
But yet it's fine because the cars we drive are never
  stalling
The reality is, we applaud reality,
When the reality is really rather appalling
This, is a superhero calling

I can't tell you all the problems of the world
Because my heart hurts
Mamma always told me,
'My son you put your heart first'
I then let my heart search
It really made my heart worse
We polluted the planet so bad
We grew to become our own curse

There are people across the world
They're really dying
There's war, there's famine, there are NGOs trying
My entire life,
There are adverts on the TV with babies that are crying
I don't vote for anybody because everybody's lying

There are animals getting killed
That we could never bring back
Photos, poses with the corpses
And who would have ever thought that?
Whilst we're stuck on this wire
I wish I was a liar

# MY PROBLEM IS I CARE TOO MUCH

Deforestation is thriving
The Amazon's on fire
They are taking the planet's lungs
To feed a corporate buyer

If you'd like to apply,
The criteria is
You don't need a cape
Or a signal in a sky
You can hide your face
We really don't care if you can't fly
You don't need a special vehicle
A theme song or a lullaby
We just really need you now
We need a superhero to come and make this right

Now all we do is share brutal things daily with each
  other
Like it can't be true
Another world crisis
Every day there's breaking news
Something has to happen
Must be something we can do
We can't just put this injustice in a place
Where everybody gets a view

We are flicking through the TV
Missing children in the channels
How dare we turn our eyes
From the truth when we travel
Lost for words
My whole life I'm playing Scrabble
The ground I have to tackle
There's so much More I have to Mackle

I pray we find solutions for the problems that arise
And everything we do, may we do it for a better life
I'm praying for our ability to give strength for the
   lives
Who really need it more than us,
Everyone deserves a chance for a peaceful life

This, is a superhero calling,
We as humanity, have dropped the ball,
But yet, we believe, we're balling,
We've lost our drive as humans
But yet it's fine because the cars we drive are never
   stalling
The reality is, we applaud reality,
When the reality is really rather appalling
This, is a superhero calling

If you'd like to apply,
The criteria is
  You don't need a cape
Or a signal in a sky
You can hide your face
We don't care if you can't fly
You don't need a special vehicle
A theme song or a lullaby
  We just really need you now
  We need a superhero to come and make this right.

# ʼVolun-tourism

He doesn't want to play your guitar babe
It doesn't matter if you got new strings
He doesn't want to play your guitar babe
It doesn't matter what sound it brings
He doesn't want to play your guitar babe

Please, he doesn't want your version of 'how to live'.

# Al-Kuhul

*The most common question I get asked when I'm out ... so*
*I thought I'd write a poem about it.*

No, I don't drink alcohol, and I don't need to explain it
Yeah , but you ...
I said I don't drink alcohol. As mentioned
I don't need to explain it.

# GRATE-FULL

*I have never eaten spaghetti or egg, and only eaten
pasta once. I hope to one day try these foods.*

I used to be ashamed for eating alone and for company I
  was seeking
When realising when I turned 30,
Food is the greatest gift and company with whom I could
  be eating.

# The Princess and Her Cave

Dearest Princess

It is not within our intention to disturb you
Whilst you lie waiting
We pray for solace of your Ancient Kingdom
Your poignant historical past
For your love
Your lover
And all that hurt you

It was never the intention for the Wild Boars to disrupt
  the peace of your spirit and its calm
Rest assured your Royal Highness
The souls of these 13 little hearts were unaware
They were so unaware

That they were soon to be swept within your dance
Now needing your chance
To go home
Just like yours
They deserve to
For you know too well
The disruption of pain caused to families
When tragedy tears them further apart

Dearest Princess
Within the realms of your majestic cave
We seek the comfort of a light from your dark

Within the request of a solemn path
So the Wild Boars can go back into their own mothers' arms

Dearest Princess.

# SWOLLEN ANKLES

It's been a long life
The arguments
His sharp tongue
The disrespect
He missed out
He failed to mention
Before you became
Husband and wife

He screams, 'Are you deaf?'
She already knows it's about to be a long night
She's working the home
Running a business
Too tired to put up a good fight
But as long as from the outside it looks all right

For this husband and wife.

# A PAGE FOR AN AGE

I was 12 when I started lyrics
I was 13 when I wish I owned a Civic
I was 14 chasing dreams to live it
I was 15 when I really tried to give it

I was 16 when I started selling tickets
I was 17 when I knew I couldn't dim it
I was 18 when doubt really tried to bring it
I was 19 when I thought I couldn't dig it

I was 20 when I really couldn't pivot
I was 21 when I knew there were no limits
22 and life started turning wicked
23 and nobody would listen

24 queuing in the clinic
25 when I wish I was playing cricket
26 when I became timid
27 I had to switch up all the digits

28 when I clocked my life's gimmick
29 and everything's moving wicked
30 and I went and binned it

I was 12 when I became a feminist
I was 13 when I had to deny I was a terrorist
I was 14 when the media was the nemesis
I was 15 rapping trying to be eloquent
I was 16 now I'm the expressionist
17 and all I got is thick hair in my inheritance
I was 18 when I clocked the world was venomous
19 I'm never fighting to be relevant

20 and my poetry is derelict
21 depressed, yeah it's really evident
22 now I'm sitting with a specialist
23 and I'm really feeling prejudiced
24 feeling like I'm on the Everest
25 never been the cleverest
26 talking to a therapist
27 can't understand my heritage
28 I become the pessimist
29 feeling the world's an experiment
30 and nothing's ever definite.

# ꟼ WANT

I want to live to see a free world
I want to live to enjoy its touch
I want to run to the edge of a mountain
And be caught by the arms of love

I want us all to walk freely amongst its land
Divine in its delicate heart
Speak to every woman as you would every man
And smile through its colourful parts

Where the mountains belong to us all
And the air is nothing but light
When nature takes her call
We're nothing but ready for the flight

I want your vibration right next to me
I want to fly with the purest dove
Live long enough to understand destiny,
I want to fall in love

Don't go for a comparative
We know where the tragic is
It's about rewriting the narrative
And finding out where the magic is

Allow yourself to be free
Of the mental chains that bound you
Reach far enough to feel something
You wouldn't normally feel around you
Only then will we know
The greatest potential of all
Our duty to share peace and love
With all around that found you.

# WAITING FOR A REPLY HOPING I DIDN'T UPSET YOU

*Being empathetic comes with many tolls. Ain't that the truth.*

All this time alone has been good
But not great for me

It's taught me too much time in my head
Means I can begin to find ways to love but also begin to
hate on me

Delving too deep within the water of empathy
Has led me to a place where I need instant reassurance
that I will not love the ones I love because it will
do a lot of pain to me

But anyway,
Enough from me,

You see there, that's what I do
I move on quickly
Bury it deep, swiftly,
On the wall, last with my emotional burden
Glad when nobody picks me

Nobody's picked me
I'm just sitting here waiting for a reply hoping I
didn't upset you
Because that in itself hits me.

# SACRIFICES

I come from the Kashmir border
From the heart of Mirpur
I am here to get a conversation started
I am here just to give a little input
When you come from the shire
Only you and Bilbo Baggins know how much of your life
  this ring took
Now I want the words printed in hardback
Because these words come from the spine of a hard book

Do you really want to know how much of me this took?
Sacrifices
I had to make
Sacrifices
Every single day
Sacrifices
To clear the way
Sacrifices
To get here today

From them East Ham back roads
Romford Road gravestones
I stand firm with my backbone
With the stem of a white rose.

# GROWING UP ON THE PAGE

When you're growing up in pain
You're growing up insane
You're growing up mental
You're growing up Hussain

When you're growing up in Ilford
You're growing up on a lane
Where your family portrait
Isn't growing in the frame

You're growing up shallow
When you're growing up in vain
But hello, meet the shrew
The one the world couldn't tame

All this fire
I'm growing up in flames
I have to thank the ones
Who were growing up in fame

When you're branded by the world
It's hard to grow up from your name
I had to change the game
When I realised I was growing up in 'BAME'

Growing up in rage
When I was growing on the stage
I grew up in the words
I grew up on the page

Who am I?
Why do you need a definition?

## MY PROBLEM IS I CARE TOO MUCH

I'm ratchet and I'm bougie
I am my only competition
You can feel the rage
Through my composition
Poetry in stadiums
Redefining tradition

I'm only really ready to follow
If I really feel your mission

My grandad's blood
Put the 'great' into Britain
Check the history,
None of this is fiction

I've found a touch
Now I've felt so many hearts
Not fazed by much
Now I carry many scars
I killed the game
Now the mandem say that I'm hard
I'm just here to play my part
I'm just an Apna Banda playing bars

Who grew up in the park
Making the fire out of sparks
Dirty always said you raise the bar up when you charge
So you better know your rights when you're speaking
    there to Sarge
And keep the street pain away from your family and your marge
My grandparents came from a village and a farm
Really very far from the sound of Notre Dame
Here's the story of the hunchback from Pakistan
Proudly singing, 'jeevay, jeevay Pakistan'

I'm here to honour and respect
My family and our past
Different kind of breed
Different kind of heart
Different kind of vision
In a different kind of class
I took a long shot
That's a different kind of pass

Real life is a special type of art
With all your missing parts
You may never find up in the charts
It's taking you afar
It's taking you to the dark
Where you really cannot dance
And on top of that
Life can be ripping you in half

Never had a sound
That felt like ours
Broken man, done way more than 10,000 hours
What did I learn through all of this?
Ghost had all the powers
Now my life is dark and black
Orange must have brought it back
Through this mirror too, I can't find my Russian doll
  in that
I'm speaking around here
The blinders chilling in the back
Not many stranger things than that.

# British-Born Confused Desi

*I was invited to go to Pakistan by the Mayor of London,*
*Sadiq Khan, to help strengthen the relationship between*
*London and Lahore. It was here I was told I was a*
*'BBCD', and everyone laughed and I didn't get it. To the*
*youth of Pakistan, I am a British-Born Confused Desi.*

I fell in love with Pakistan,
Even though I am your British-Born Confused Desi, you
  are still meri jaan,
I've fallen in love with everything about you and it
  starts with tere naam,
So my heart sings 'jeevay, jeevay', whilst my soul sings
  'Pakistan'

But certain world media doesn't like us,
They like to pick at our place,
Say it's a confused state, oh what a hell of a place,

But you have to come here to feel it,
And I've felt a lot,
From Jhelum to Islamabad I still need to visit Sialkot

So when I was on PIA heading here,
I was smiling, because I am a student of Benazir,

Ready to smell sugarcane and guava,
I am four provinces, I am one army,
I am the pride of my father,

I fell in love with Pakistan,
And even though I am your British-Born Confused Desi,
  you are still meri jaan,

 91

I've fallen in love with everything about you and it
  starts with tere naam,
So my heart sings 'jeevay, jeevay', whilst my soul sings
  'Pakistan'

It was every time Nusrat shocked the world the moment he
  moved his lips,
Every time Afridi changed the game and hit the ball for
  a six
Every time you remember Malala was just a kid,
Every time you remember what Abdul Sattar Edhi taught
  us, you don't need to have a lot to give to have a lot
  to give,

It's that Karachi smell
Them Lahoree nights
The beauty of Muzaffarabad
The people of Rawalpindi's plight

I am every child's lost voice,
Every mother's forgotten pain
Every construction worker's height,
I am everything that will never be the same,

I fell in love with Pakistan,
And it started with Dr Abdus Salam,
And the teachings of Iqbal,
So even though I am your British-Born Confused Desi, you
  will always be meri jaan,

We've got a lot of work to do,
But we done well,
We've only been around for 70 years and we fought
  through hell,

Through the zakat that's given,
Pakistan is the haat that's risen,
Against all odds,
It's now time we push our children on top,

I fell in love with Pakistan,
And even though I am your British-Born Confused Desi,
  you are still meri jaan,
I've fallen in love with everything about you and it
  starts with tere naam,
So my heart sings 'jeevay, jeevay', whilst my soul sings
  'Pakistan'.

## Chapter Three

# THE NIGHT OF 31 AUGUST 2017

It's 28 December 2021, and I am currently in Los
Angeles, California. Casting my mind back to when my
mother was alive, one recurring theme always hits me
when it comes to her: she never actually saw me perform
live once. She wasn't really into performing arts,
cinema, film or television, but when something moved
her, it really did. To give you a fine example, out of
26 years of being with my mother, we only went to the
cinema once and that was to watch *Kabhi Khushi Kabhie
Gham* at the legendary Boleyn Cinema in East Ham near
Grandma's house.

There was something that made her super nervous;
even when it came to me being on television, online or
whatever it was, she would never watch or engage. She
would ask my siblings how it was, or she would text me
and ask if people liked it or whether anyone had even
turned up. When my friends came round she would ask them
how it was and quickly move on to another subject, but
it was never done with any form of malice; if anything,
it was really cute.

She became nervous for me. I, on the other hand, was
walking around with that Beyoncé energy believing I was
destined for this. It was quite the situation. I had
booked my first live show - my first solo, proper live
show with a full band, stage, lights and everything.
It was at a new music venue in Central London by Tower
Bridge called OMEARA. It had a capacity of 300 people
and it was sold out! The show was set to be on 21
November 2017.

I remember Mum saying to me that she would come and
watch me one day when she felt like it was the right
thing to do, and one day I came home from wherever I was
and she told me that she had purchased a new dress and
it was hanging in the small box room upstairs. She told

me she'd bought this dress for when she comes to watch
me perform at OMEARA. My heart was full, I was so happy;
I could not believe something had persuaded her to come
and watch me. I was so thrilled.

'I'm not cooking tonight, it's my night off. I'm
going to order a pizza - can you pay for it?' my mum
said to me as I was getting ready to leave the house
to see a very close friend of mine on the night of 31
August 2017.

I replied, 'I have no money on me' and headed
towards my car. I was so preoccupied with seeing my
friend and not wanting to be late that I completely
disregarded my mother's wish. Luckily, I sat in my car
on the driveway and automatically felt this insane,
overwhelming feeling of guilt.

I got out of the car and went back inside and said
to Mum, 'I'm going to transfer it to you now by online
banking,' and she replied, 'No it's OK, thank you. I
I'm glad you offered to pay for it.' I told her I'd see
her soon and left the house. Little did I know what was
in store for me that night. I was just very glad and
grateful I went back in and offered to pay.

My mother was an incredible cook and takeaways were
normally reserved for Friday nights in our house. She
always cooked with so much love and made sure whenever
any of our friends came to our home that they ate, and
they ate good!

I'd just arrived at my best friend's house. We were
sitting on his sofa watching some random television
show, just talking about absolutely nothing, but that's
what best friends do - you can just sit there with each
other and the time goes by, but it's all good.

It must have been past 10pm when my dad called me
and said, 'Mum's fainted, you should come home.' I was

instantly like, 'What do you mean, "Mum's fainted"? Give her the phone - I will get her up', and he said, 'No, come home.'

I got off the phone, looked at my best friend and said to him, 'I think my mum has passed away' and he told me not to say that. I literally ran out of his flat and into my car, and from Bethnal Green hit the A406 past Stratford's Olympic Park, past Leytonstone train station and by this point I was crying; I knew something was not right.

There was something in the atmosphere that was not sitting well with me, so I decided to call someone very close to me who happened to live a few doors down from my family home, and I asked him to go to my house and give the phone to my mum. I kept him on the phone and I heard him ring the doorbell and my dad answered and said to him, 'You can't come in today'. It was soul-shaking to hear this - this was not common at all.

I turned into my road to see four ambulances, the neighbours outside, the front door wide open and every house light on. It was around 11pm when I walked in through the front door. Beside her prayer mat, there she was; lying peacefully. The paramedics did an incredible job. We were all in the room - me, my siblings, my dad - and we watched as my mum's soul drifted into another realm.

It was cold but warm; it was heartbreaking but soothing; it was devastating but calming. She looked at so much peace. At this point; we were unaware of what had caused her death, but shortly later we learnt that it was a brain aneurysm. So quick, so sudden. Mum hadn't been to the doctor in 15 years. She was as fit as a working mum of four could be and in the best space mentally and spiritually she had ever been in.

I remember the paramedics had been trying to bring her back for around 45 minutes and I told them they could stop. They apologised and I said, 'It's OK, there's no need to. It was her time to go, and plus my little sister is a nurse so if anyone was to save her it would be her.'

The hardest moment that was to follow was to make the phone calls to our family (her sisters and brothers) and inform them of the news. Everyone lives within such close proximity and was at our house within minutes. My grandmother arrived (my father's mother), my aunties, uncles, cousins; everyone who loved her was there. She was in her beautiful home, she was lying by her prayer mat, she was at peace. It was a moment I will never - and can never - forget.

I never had a chance to tell my mum I loved her. I never had any form of opportunity to say goodbye. I never was able to show her any of my successes, but little did I know I was about to restart my life without my best friend, my main number one, my everything by my side. It was a really sad, hard and difficult moment, and even writing this now reflecting back on it I can't believe we managed to get through it.

I took everything she taught me and left me with and began writing instantly.

This was the hardest chapter of my life. And after four and half years of dealing with our grief, I am ready to share the poems that saved me through the most turbulent moment of my life.

For as long as we possibly could, we let Mum's dress hang on the wall in the small box room of our house in its see-through bag. What she may never have known is that it laid against my first ever writings I did with my older sister of 'Lyrical Gangsta'. I guess it's poetic justice after all.

I present to you, Chapter Three:

The Night of 31 August 2017.

# THE WHITE ROSE

You're the one God took home
I miss you
no matter what they say
I miss you
I've never missed anyone the way I miss you
The moment you left, our house doesn't smell the same
our doorbell doesn't ring your name
our home phone doesn't buzz for days
and our names don't mean our names
To the Lord in the sky
the day you took one of your creations back
I guess we had to return what you gave us
the deepest thanking you for that
but please allow the angels to take care of her
she's fragile and that
but she'd never admit it around us,
no, she was bigger than that
she had banter too
a proper East End laugh
the first of her kind
the East End ammi jaan
In my head every moment's raw
I don't know what you was Mum
But you was everything and more
I'm just grateful for them 26 years and everything I saw
All the love you gave me
How in my hardest times you aid me
you made me and shaped me
bathed me and saved me
it's pretty clear to see, I'm very proud to say my mum
  raised me
a white rose by your grave is my heart to you

I call myself the Original Mummy's Boy because that is
  my love for you
this right here,
is somehow my mum for you
even when she's gone she's given me this honour
told me when you do it, Hussain, do it proper
if you think your desires are hot
hell's hotter
and you're not doing it,
I'm not having it,
none of my kids are ever going to skydive out of a
  chopper
I love you Mum
wherever you are, when people who don't know ask
I say it's in Heaven you are
whenever you are
thinking to pop back
the door's always open
the kitchen will be clean
I know she'd be hoping
but I love you Mum
I am not joking
how I somehow morphed into a little version of you
for the first time in my life
the hopeless one has started hoping
But I gotta go now
the bathroom window needs closing
I need to get the iron on the clothing
clean the bathroom floor; Dad left it soaking
I'm just here to follow in your path
remember how happy you got when we went to B&Q and
  bought a table and chairs
for your garden and grass
I never got the chance to sit by a campfire with you

or take you to lunch at The Ritz
you never got to see me get married
and you will never see one of my kids
but all you wanted to do was see me live
I guess, here I am
It's because of you
I hope to God right now, wherever you are standing,
  somehow I manage to get in front of you
even though you can't see me anymore, I still want to
  tell you I belong to you
but I guess she left earth when her kids were ready as
  she always used to say things happen overdue
so good night Mum
you too son
take care my boy
Mum, listen, wherever you are, I hope you get the chance
  to relax and enjoy
I can't sit still and neither can you
and just know, whatever I do I will for you
I just pray to God I get to see you soon x

# AMMI'S HAAT

The warmth of my mother's hands
Transformed my pain into a peaceful land

I miss the warmth of my mother's hands.

# THE MORNING AFTER YOU LEFT

*The only thing I have of my mother's to this day is the
kitchen chair I last saw her sitting on.*

You are truly unforgettable
My beautiful mum
How everything I loved
Has now gone
My insides numb
My phone line drums
It's like the sky losing its sun

You are truly unforgettable
My beautiful mum

I wish my brain would automatically save
Our conversations that surpassed timeless hours
All I do now is pray the Lord expands your grave
And you are blessed with heavenly powers

I've stopped questioning, 'Why did you have to go?'
Because I guess you raised me better
I hope it's all right with you,
I tell the world the story of how you left
I read it from my soul,
As if your departure was a love letter
As the pain got deeper
The story only got better
As your signs only got stronger
That's why it's impossible to ever forget her

For a few years I thought your death had done me though
I was screaming on the floor,

Crying
Saying it's done me bro
But I've learnt how to respond to pain
Now when it comes knocking,
I say, 'Welcome in, off we go'

Please don't worry Mum,
You don't need to get a flight back
I've got on your light
I am more than ready to fight back
If I end up going a little left
Your prayers will ensure I'm right back
Please, believe, if life throws me a few curveballs
I will be ready to throw life some curveballs right back

I'm part-time psycho
That weren't no typo
Your tea's gone cold,
I'm not wondering why
I'm refusing to ever let you die-doe

Life through me, deep baggage
I had to do a crash course in learning to control damage
I guess you partnered me with pain before you left

The irony of you always wanting me to have an arranged
    marriage

I guess, that's the best match
We lost our queen,
Life's gone a little bit harder
The king alone is still capable of winning a chess match
I got sent a delivery of pain in a fresh batch
But by this point

I've acclimatised well enough to really manoeuvre
  amongst the rules of the game of life in its test
  match

You are truly unforgettable
My beautiful mum
How everything I loved
Has now gone
My insides numb
My phone line drums
It's like the sky losing its sun

You are truly unforgettable
My beautiful mum

When I look up I feel empty
They say you're still with me
I say, 'Please don't say that; I really want to join
  her,
'Don't tempt me'

But everything you taught me
Life and its lessons
Are beginning to answer the pain and its questions
And even though it's just rain and depression
I'm going to stay for this session

Now certain people are telling me,
'You need to move on slowly
'Get religious bruv,
'You need to move on, holy'
I'm just planning to stand here and defend your honour
Mum, I am your lifetime goalie

It's so hard to accept and digest that you are never
  going to phone me
Or when I am ill
Touch my head and hold me
Mum I'm lonely
All these people around me
But none of them know me

See, I did it again
I put myself into a hole
I did it again
Away from my friends
So I can dwell in my silence and pity

Don't worry Ammi,
When I am mentally back
I am going to make the world my city
With a flow that's witty
A style that's gritty
Full of pain

But somehow this Mummy's Boy will make the pain look
  pretty
You are truly unforgettable
My beautiful mum
How everything I loved
Has now gone
My insides numb
My phone line drums
It's like the sky losing its sun

You are truly unforgettable
My beautiful mum.

# Nothing Without You, Mum

When you left you took my heart
You was everything in my future
How am I meant to accept
You are about to become everything in my past?
You saw me go from first grade to first class
Now you have left
I feel as if I have to go back to my first grade and,
  without you, I have no idea on how I can resit my
  first class

It was not meant to be like this
These tests were not meant to last
You was meant to see me spread my poems all over the world
You was meant to see me fly to Mars

Now I am sitting here screaming
Ammi Jaan
Dua mein yaad
I have nothing besides me
Nothing to comfort
Nothing to hide me
Just talk to me once more, mere baat
Sit here with me please, mere saat

I couldn't believe it, your funeral prayer
Filled the park
Sab ke bandeh tere pass

I will build the wells you aimed for
I will live the dreams you prayed for
I never knew in life what I was made of,
But I know this is what I was made for

So blessed, I have never seen a person look more alive
  when they looked dead
So for me what's next?
I guess whatever seems appealing
But me and the world have a lot in common
We both need a lot of healing
My name is Hussain
Now it's time for me to understand its meaning.

# I Got Through One Night

I got through one night
I got through three and four
I've got through a couple more
Now I need to get through a couple more
Go through and Heaven's yours

I'm sat crying through the nights
So I can smile at Heaven's doors
I heard Heaven's got seven floors,
That's where my mum is,
Or she's at least by the gates looking in,

I want to be able to make it so I can run up and scream
  and say, 'Mum, it's Hussain. I made it in, they let
  me in'
But Mum, we had a rule and you broke it,
You said we never leave the house without greeting
  everyone, you know this,
Even in work when you leave you have to hand in your
  notice,
I've learnt you can be so full of grief and still be
  soulless,
You made our home a house; you made our home without
  you - homeless,

I was full of hope and now I don't know what hope is,
I know my character's plot twist but I can't figure out
  his motive

Everyone says if you need someone to speak to,
But this is something for the phone
This is a piece of my mind

In my state of time
When my hate's inclined at the peakest time
To destroy my weaker side,
Bruv this ain't even the deepest tide, this is an easy
  night.

I'm trying to start the healing,
But the truth starts revealing,
My insides are bleeding,
Because everything in there is fighting, everything's
  its feelings,

So Hussain please just write
Let it make sense on paper, please just type,
It will make sense in decent time
My mind's in pieces
What did you expect?
I lost the biggest piece of mind

I'm writing in seconds over pages when my mind's in
  the motion
Mum, they're printing the story of my grief on four
  pages, my mind's in the notion
I feel it all over my body, my mind's in the lotion
I'm the lifeguard trying to fight my own tsunami, my
  mind's lost at sea in the ocean

I'm glad I come from you and your blessed hands
But I've built a couple of sandcastles on lands made out
  of quicksand
Trying to go punch for punch, bar for bar,
I learnt in order to survive
I need to have quick hands
I got so many people standing with me,

All this drama is something I can withstand

When I go visit Mum, I pray I hope you're resting good
I try to project it in the ground for her to incorporate
  my sound
I don't know if it's some deep stuff,
Or if these words will ever make it down,
And all I hear now is tractors and diggers
Building homes for the saints and the sinners
There are two types of people at the graveyard:
Losers and winners.

# Praying for Clarity and Sanity

I'm in the graveyard
Praying for clarity
I should be praying for Mum
But I'm praying for sanity
Hoping she's not mad at me
But I hear her say,

*Just be my son for me,*
*hurry up son,*
*your life on earth is short,*
*your time's tight,*
*your hair's changing colour because your life's full of*
  *highlights,*
*your heart's been broken because your love is full of*
  *bye byes,*
*but understand Hussain,*
*when you let a piece of you die,*
*that's when I die.*

# How Do I Post a Letter to Heaven?

Oh it's happening
Through the drama and the pain
Oh it's happening
Through the trajectory of my fight I can feel it
  happening
You said the world will see my smile
I say, 'Mum, it's happening'


Everything I saved up I lost
Everything you prayed for I got
Just so I can feel you shout at me I still wear stains
  on my top
I can still hear you say, 'Get home now, the kitchen's
  closed, your house ain't a hotel'
don't worry Mum, I still ain't forgot
I listened to N-Dubz so much
not knowing my story would too go against all odds
but it did, and somehow I am still standing
They tell me to stand straight, get your back up
But over here Mum they just call it branding
I never thought you'd be the one to make me stand out
But now with your blessings there's so much I'm handling
I wear my heart on my chest
That is all that's visible
It's got a dagger in the middle
In a story that's killable
I'm just leading the way out
I've got just got a couple smart syllables
I didn't hit the nail on the head
I'm smashing it with a bolt that's drillable
because I've learnt to give away my emotions
I let the world have them for free

I let the planet take every little thing, but the one
  thing it won't be taking is me
Keep sending me letters from Heaven
I'll just keep replying to the sky
Keep the space next to you for me
Let them know your son will take his time
when he's here you'll know
I'll grab the pearly gates and scream, 'Mum, I'm home'
it's been ages,
I've gone through stages
I wrote the story down I knew they wouldn't let me bring
  in my pages
but it's in my mind
I've saved it there
protecting it from this world, because they're trying to
  tell me I am not sane over here
but where I'm at now
Hussain's OK over here
I walk through our empty home
where you've left memories in the walls
I take my time blowing the candles for every memory that
  was born
IG1 threading me stitches as I've got a couple of
  memories that were torn
but everything you taught me,
they're the memories that I've worn
Oh it's happening
Through the drama and the pain
Oh it's happening
Through the trajectory of my fight I can feel it
  happening
And you said the world will see my smile
I say, 'Mum, it's happening.'

# THE FIRST SIX MONTHS

Half a year became an emotional marathon
Full of mayhem
One I never signed up for running

In my car
I'd drive aimlessly crying and screaming
Really hoping
For the touch of my mother
Or a note from Heaven
Or just something

People stopped coming round
The house became so quiet
I couldn't sit in the silence
As my head would begin to riot

Everyone moved on faster
Guess I'm stuck in the mud
But having done nearly five years without you Ammi Jaan
I'm really glad in the first six months I never gave up.

# HOME-COOKED FOOD

*I still need to learn how to cook, but I've been putting
it off as this is a huge reality check that my mother is
no longer here. She was an amazing cook. However, today
I did buy a crusty roll and made myself a sandwich with
salt and vinegar crisps inside, of course!*

Nothing sings true unless the song was you
Nothing rings new now that my life is blue
Nothing ain't true, it don't matter how I do
Because I can't smell you in my home-cooked food

I order lazy food
Food I order by clicking
My mouth's not watering and my fingers I'm not licking
I stand by the microwave
Just to press it open
I put my hands in
But my problems I can't solve them

You see, I can write dreams
But I can't cook
And that's a hard read up in my book
Because what my life seems,
My life took
And there's not really a healthy recipe up in my book

Nothing sings true unless the song was you
Nothing rings new now that my life is blue
Nothing ain't true, it don't matter how I do
Because I can't smell you in my home-cooked food.

# I THINK MY MUM'S FORGOT ME :'(

*There are various stages of grief; for me, one of them*
*is anger and nobody wants to talk about this because*
*nobody wants to openly admit that they are angry at the*
*person they love for leaving them.*

I call my older sister
I say, 'I think Mum forgot me.
'It's been five years - why hasn't she come and got me?'

There are things in my way
A couple things are trying to stop me
Mum, I know you hated us watching and playing wrestling
But, right now, The Rock has really got me
Dad's always saying that it's nice where you are
But I need you back Mum,
Heaven is just too far
I am screaming up there too
I send packages for you
I wrap them up in prayers
with all that's happened in there too
You see, the moment that you left us
a part of me got killed
now I am shouting and I am angry
I am not taking up the deal
why on earth did you leave your family?
Someone please tell me this ain't real
and how are they saying I am not manly just because I am
  saying how I feel?
I don't even have a new number
but why won't Heaven let you call me?
I guess it's just me, then, when I'm lonely
just please tell me you haven't forgot me

I don't even have a new number
but why won't Heaven let you call me?
I guess it's just me, then, when I'm lonely
just please tell me you haven't forgot me.

# There's No More Moments

I guess it's a long way to call me
I'm guessing it's a longer way to go
But whoever is in Heaven with you, my mother
I want to let them know
that there's not a moment I'm not thinking
of how you was at home
that there's not a moment I'm not thinking
you might just ring my phone
I can read the stories and the scriptures
I can leave my pain between the lines
but if you loved me so much, tell me something
why did you leave me behind?
Many moments haunt me,
I go deep with what I find
but all of these moments taught me
There's really no good, in goodbye
I guess it's a long way to call me
I'm guessing it's a longer way to go
But whoever is in Heaven with you, my mother
I want to let them know
that there's not a moment I'm not thinking
of how you was at home
that there's not a moment I'm not thinking
you might just ring my phone
All of life hits harder
now that you're not near
but your child is smarter
and you always knew it was there

Certain nights I wake up crying
trapped in a hole
if you really love me tell me something

will you ever come home?
I guess it's a long way to call me
I'm guessing it's a longer way to go
But whoever is in Heaven with you, my mother
I want to let them know
that there's not a moment I'm not thinking
of how you was at home
that there's not a moment I'm not thinking
you might just ring my phone
I guess it's a long way to call me
I'm guessing it's a longer way to go
But whoever is in Heaven with you, my mother
I want to let them know
that there's not a moment I'm not thinking
of how you was at home
that there's not a moment I'm not thinking
you might just ring my phone.

# IF SHE WAS HERE

If she was here
I would tell her I missed her
I would tell her when the ambulance came and we carried
  you out of the house
I pushed through the sheet they put over her and on her
  forehead I kissed her

If she was here,
I'd tell her,
The night you left Mum, I got thrown into a twister
And I just wish I could go back to them days I would
  come home from school and sit on the sofa and you'd
  tell me to hurry up,
It was *My Wife & Kids*,
*Saved By the Bell*,
I better eat my yoghurt with *Kenan & Kel*, Tia and Tamera
  in *Sister, Sister*

If she was here
The bricks to our home wouldn't have fallen
If she was here
My drive wouldn't have got lost,
My engine wouldn't have stallen
If she was here
I never would have wrote these words,
But now it's just the words I have that turn to prayers
  that I hope are calling

Your heart line
But I don't expect you to come to Heaven's frontline
And look down, but if you do get some time
Maybe if you could Mum, just look, one time

And see we're getting through grief just fine
I hope you got to see your sunshine
Not to say I'm not hurting
But not letting the hurt of you consume all of time
Because that's not what you wanted
To live and occupy both heart and mind

And you know,
In my heart is where I keep you
my mind is where we speak to
sometimes it's so hard for me to accept it,
even harder when sometimes I can't feel you
Then I feel guilty then overwhelm myself
Stand still and breathe through

But I guess this is what growth looks like and if you
    ever see me on a day like this Mum,
It basically means it doesn't matter how strong I look
I still want to see you

If she was here

I would tell her I missed her
I would tell her when the ambulance came and we carried
    you out of the house I pushed through that sheet they
    put over you Mum and on her forehead I kissed her
I can never forget what she left inside of me

But I miss her
She was a special gift her
A good mother,
Is the pillar of the home
The operation and the base
Strapped with epic one-liners

And can shut you down just from pulling a look on
  her face

Flying up and down the stairs no matter what the age
Telling you, you can really do it, even when every odd
  is against you in the race

If she was here

She'd put me in my place

I realised I will get married without your presence
And that is an excruciating pain, an overwhelming
  essence
I learnt so much you said that became true when you
  passed
I learnt so many new lessons
I still remember what you taught me though,
I'm still holding closely on to your blessings
And the home-cooked food, as hard as we try, no one's
  touching your dressings

Mother's Day without your mother
True say can be really hard
But what I learnt is what they left us with
The love and blessings
It's only yours, it's only ours
And sometimes that's enough to get through
You let it out,
You don't ever keep the way you're feeling her in jars

If she was here

I would tell her I missed her
I would tell her when the ambulance came and we carried
  you out of the house I pushed through that sheet they
  put over you Mum and on her forehead I kissed her

If she was here

I'd tell her, her grandchildren stand by her grave with
  watering cans,
Asking all the questions in the world about their
  wonderful nan
But what hurts the most is you don't get to see how much
  of you is in them
But there's so much that I don't understand
She loved you so much and still does; can you feel it?
  I can

Life without you can seem impossible
But day by day will make it probable
Honourable, we're growing up now we're responsible
Through every day, through every obstacle

Because she still is here
A mother's love is unstoppable.

# Dear Diary

Dear diary,
I was young on a Sega Mega Drive
When my mum used to pray
I, naive and dumb
And my mum used to say,
'It's OK, go to bed, you don't worry about that today'

Now you're gone,
I write poems Mum, to hold all my pain
The best thing you ever gave to me
Was my name
Now I'm broken-hearted,
Travelling across the world,
Telling the people in the mental struggle,
My name is Hussain

When life thunderstormed on me
I had to teach myself how to dance in the rain
Rock bottom,
The story from the cradle near missing the grave

Dear diary,
I've had better days,
I've dealt with all my different pain in different ways
And even though I'm not, I'm still the same
I don't run to fame
I was a Bat in a Cave and in walked in Bane

Looked at me like a challenger
But I ain't no amateur
I been here since Pamela
Now when I shoot my calibre

They shoot me with a camera
To tell you the truth dear diary,
The only thing I've seen fall better than me is Niagara
I let my water fall, riding waves of stamina
But Mum I miss your touch
I miss your laugh
I miss how you was the only one who knew how to fix me
    and my brother and sister's broken parts
When you left,
Can't you see you took all the pieces that would fix my
    broken heart?
Mum, doesn't Heaven let you see I have a broken heart?
Can't you see that my heart is broken?
I can't feel you where you are Mum, and that's why even
    my hope is hoping
Nobody is telling me that my life's joking

And nobody gets to see me when I'm not coping
Having learnt when you stop dancing in the rain, that's
    when you realise your life's soaking

But I know if you was here you'd say one thing to me
That's keep going, you keep going
You get up, you show the world you can keep going
Life's a stream, so get on your boat and keep rowing,

The show must go on you keep showing
You keep going
You keep going.

# THE BEST YEARS

*You really are having the best years of your life when
you don't realise you are having the best years of your
life.*

I still walk with you by my side
wearing everything you taught me I will not hide: my
  scars, my wounds, my broken eyes,
I don't tell anybody about the nights I cry,
where I pray and hide
because it's you Mum I find
who gave me the best years of my life
now that is with me,
everywhere I go
when desire and distraction step in,
somehow you're still there,
at every single no
I can't let you go
and it kills me that I can't let you know
I think about writing more letters Mum,
sending them to the sky
I think about what you'd say if you came to see me here
  tonight
I think of all the moments
I think of all the times
my friends say I'm overthinking because I'm thinking all
  the time of the best years of my life
which were the best years of time
those were the best years of our lives
I will forever keep them all in mind
it's how you said more when you spoke less
you had a touch that could shine things
that famous line 'the night is for rest'

your superwoman ability to find things
you'd attack me with a sponge
clean the stains off my clothes
you'd be at the front door fast
there was no way bad energy was entering the home
you see your best years,
are the years your dear mum phones
and she tells you to leave the lights on because there's
  no one home
when the phone rings answer,
tell them your mum's not home
the best years of your lives are the years your mum
  doesn't leave you alone
now I'm so scared to let love in Mum,
I'm so scared to see what will happen
I can't even listen to Destiny's Child
and life wants me to trust destiny's pattern
but my best years stopped
the moment your heart line flattened
because my life was shattered
now the internet asks me why you battered
I lost my best friend, I tell them, there
that's a bit of content, that's what happened,
but I'm fighting through it
I'm pushing through
because if it's one thing I saw,
I saw you go through it too
how you spoke when your dad left
I was there when your mum left
but I never understood what it meant to live in a world
where there's no mum left
but now I know, yes,
and look we're making progress
it's so hard but Mum I know you know this

the best years of my life,
with you, the best years of time
those were the best years of our lives
I forever keep them all in mind.

# LIVING A 'LIFE' WITHOUT YOU

You was right Mum
When your parents leave, nobody cares
I cry at night Mum
And you know what?
There's nobody there
But Mum I know you're near
And because of that I'm not scared

I just want you to tell me what it's like over there,
If you're all right over there
Because I know if I ask you,
You will ask me,
And right now, I'm not all right over here
You'd open my door at a specific speed
Ready with the ability to handle every need
Knowing what it was without me having to speak
Knowing when I'm awake and when I'm meant to be asleep
You knew I wasn't smart enough to cheat
Which is why you saw me break at every defeat
But you never gave me the cheat
Because you knew I could do it
The moment you left
I began to pursue it
Now every night Mum I get through it
I just take my time
I don't even ask God why
I just pray and say, 'Please somehow tell her I'm fine'

I know if it's hurting me
It's hurting you
Then it's not just me
There are the rest of us too

And I can hear you saying, 'It's OK Hussain, go to sleep
  now, remember the world is going to see your smile'
Well, tell you the truth Mum, I haven't smiled in a
  while
I put on a mask for a bit
I gave that a trial, but it's no good living in denial

I know you're there to heal me
I'm just saying it out loud
I know if I moved out of line you'd still kill me
Which is why I keep the noise down
Everything I do, I do so the people feel me
I'm just trying to make you proud
In my heart I know you still love me

I guess I don't really need you to say it now x

# 1,095 DAYS

That is three whole years
And from when you left after the first couple of days
  the world moved on
I learnt one thing quickly, unintentionally and not
  maliciously, but no one cares
If you're lucky someone might randomly call
But truth be told, no one's there
I miss your presence in the night and to tell you the
  truth I'm scared
Of what a future looks like without you
When the family portrait no longer bounds you
It's not my noise in the house that reaches you and
  hounds you
I've never been more jealous of those in the afterlife
  who get to surround you
Because you left me in the heartbreak and grief came and
  drowned you
I can't move on without knowing answers to certain
  questions
Life doesn't allow you
To feel the crown you
Left above my head but I know it's there
Mother I don't doubt you.

# DAWN

I nearly didn't wake up
I nearly really missed you
I nearly slept through the clock
I nearly really dismissed you

I nearly couldn't believe it
I nearly really was tricked too

Not waking up at dawn to pray for all of the parts of
you I miss too.

# FRIDGE MAGNETS

We have fridge magnets
Of the places everyone's been
And it's all you ever said to bring back,
That and ourselves

We have The O2, next to Professor Burp's Bubbleworks,
And some dodgy key rings that broke but you hid them
  behind your nice cutlery, never threw them away on
  your shelves

I got to see Notre Dame today
F. P. took me to see Mbappe score

But what's hit hard in my tourist hour

Is the fact that I didn't stop at the man with his
  products on the floor on a blanket to buy a key ring
  for you from when I finally saw the Eiffel Tower.

# ONE DAY

We'll all be together in Heaven
Past the diamond gates
At the dinner table full of love and care,
Having alleviated every form of depression
Where time is kind and it no longer makes us wait
As we feel the reward of the hard work that leads to a
  peaceful internal progression

One day, we'll be reunited
With our dearest loved ones,
Our hearts once again will be excited
One day, we will be alive in the words that caught the
  tears from our eyes
That we spent wishing, praying whilst writing
Destiny will be present,
One day, we will no longer be fighting

One day, we would have paid the price as we say goodbye
  to our vice,
One day, we will feel the surprise, of the sunshine,
  arise, from cloud nine,
Divine in its delight, sending the sound of butterflies,
  to mesmerise our broken hearts as they finally become
  healed in paradise

One day,
Some way,
One may,
Head up to Heaven
On the runway
And ask which way
My mum stays,
One day,
One day.

# MUM TOLD ME WHEN SHE IS NOT HERE TO CRY AND GET OVER IT

*The most valuable bit of life advice that Mum gave me.*

Ammi Jaan if you're listening
I'm by your grave and it's glistening
I'm praying and I'm saying
I will never give up wishing

When I lost you Mum
Grief started thickening
A battle that is crippling
Plenty moments that are sickening

I had to start life again or life restarted
They left your role out and it was never recasted
I don't soul-trade, I just freelance it
I learnt to be a hustler from you in the market

My hands are really shaking when I was there holding
  your casket
I got so many questions and to God I will have to ask it
Now when I'm in my room first thing I have to do
Is close the curtains, to write my poetry I really have
  to dark it

You lost your dad early
You lost your mum later
You were the winner of the arguments and the peacemaker
Went back to Pakistan
To buy us all a couple acre
No woman ever greater
You shoulda seen where it'd take her

We're in zoos across the world fighting for animal rights
Summers in the villages, we're really learning life
How you kept so much from us Mum,
That thing about you, was something I really didn't like

My career took a while Mum, I know it really did
But you eased the pressure when you said
Depression will not win
So I won the battle through it
When I gave it everything

But you never got to see us go
You never got to see a show
Mum, they're standing up in every single row
Thailand and Colombia, we're booked all round the globe
Your prayer so strong
I never feel I'm on my own

I now can see why you prayed a lot
Looking back, I can see it in your mind
Because me versus the world
Is me versus evil eye
That's a battle all my life
With your prayers it's a battle I can fight
Now when it overstays its welcome
I push it off my mind
I pray through the nights
I cry, I have to cry

Now I'm really looking into how you said goodbye.

# ONE MILLION TIMES / YOU HAVE MY WORD

I will walk the path of one million miles
I will search the folder of one million files
I will stand and give evidence in one million trials
If it means I've taken a step closer to you

Mum, you don't need to worry, you have my word

I will scheme one million schemes
I will plead one million pleads
I will redeem all of what I can redeem
If it means I've taken a step closer to you

Mum, you don't need to worry, you have my word

I will write one million lines
I will try one million times
I will save one million dimes
If it means I've taken a step closer to you

Mum, you don't need to worry, you have my word

I will stay awake through the violence and silence
And pray through the quietness of one million nights
Whilst fighting the fight that comes with the fight of
   the one million fights
Just to get closer to one single sight, of you

Mum, you don't need to worry, you have my word

I don't know how, but I will find one million ways
I will live as if I have only today
Whilst living as if I have one million days

To be around you for a single stay
If it means I've taken a step closer to you

Mum, you don't need to worry, you have my word

I will sacrifice what's left of my whole life
To feel your love just one single time
If it means I'll set sight
On your loving set of eyes
If it means I get to become closer to you

Mum, you don't need to worry, you have my word

I will run my little feet across one million roads
Carrying with me
My complex grief
In its million loads
Just to know you'd be home
If it means I get to become closer to you

Mum, you don't need to worry, you have my word

I will believe what I have to believe
If it means I get to sit in your peace
Whilst I read the lines of one million signs
Descending from the Heavens from one million skies
Even if it takes my whole life
Just to speak to you one single time
I will not rest, I will not sleep
If it means I get to become closer to you
Mum, you don't need to worry, you have my word

I will write one million verses
I will pray against one million curses

I will go and find one million nurses
If it means I get to become closer to you

Mum, you don't need to worry, you have my word

One million times I will beat depression
One million times I will annoy anxiety out of its
  succession
One million times I will find a way to write one million
  suggestions
If it means I get to become closer to you

Mum, you don't need to worry, you have my word

I will find one million threads
I will find one million needles
To stitch my broken heart, because it cannot rest
I will search amongst the crowd of one million people
If it means I get to become closer to you

Mum, you don't need to worry, you have my word

I will understand but refuse to understand that love
  again may never be equal
I will tie my love letters to the wings of one million
  eagles
I will do what I can to overcome one million nightmares
And I will pray to overthrow one million evils
If it means I get to become closer to you

Mum, you don't need to worry, you have my word
You have my word.

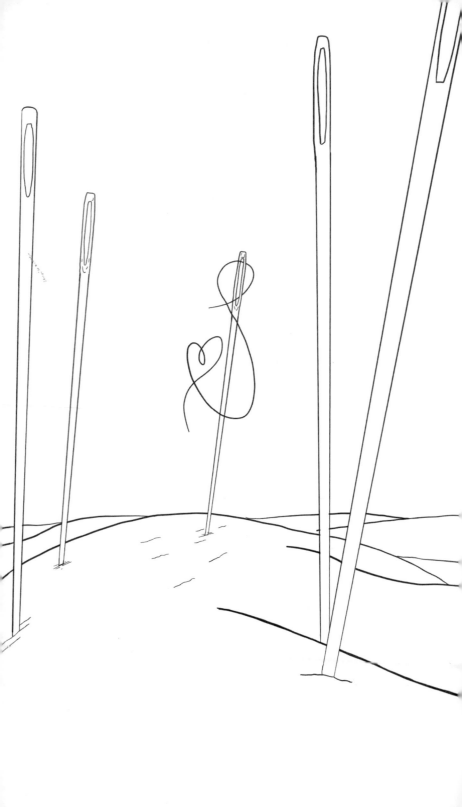

# 49

Eternally blissful and young
I guess you was never meant to have any white hair,
Any teeth loss
I guess you was never meant to grow old
As you left happy, daring, carefree and young
I still remember everything you taught me
Written across my soul in bold

No doubt, wherever you are,
You're dancing to the beat of your own drum
The absolute pillar, queen and foundation of the
  household
Thankful, it was in your life I had the utmost privilege
  to be enrolled
Thank you for making me your son

Sometimes I do feel done
Outspun
No fight left in me
Angry to myself, for everything I didn't become
Numb, glum, bit by bit I begin to crumb,
All because I keep replaying in my mind she was 49
When she was called to Heaven

I'm conflicted with agreeing and disagreeing
It was the right time or you was too young
49,
She was
49
My dear mum.

# FRIDAY NIGHTS ON ILFORD LANE

Mum would say,
'OK hurry up,
'I can't park here
'Go inside I've ordered it on the phone
'Tell them you're here'

We'd order food by selecting numbers off a wall
Starting at meal number 1 going into double digits
Once selected, you'd wait on the stalls

Salt and pepper
Ketchup and sauce that's chilli
Mum always said one fizzy drink a week
Or your teeth will rot, and your smile will look silly

Back in the car
We'd rush home
EastEnders on at 8
We'd all sit there
Not one of us on a 'smart device' or phone

Friday night our takeaway day from Ilford Lane
Were the best nights of my life,
I'd give anything for them, I'd trade
Just to hear my mum shout,
'OK do the dishes, turn the kitchen lights off, now go
  to bed Hussain' x

# BECAUSE, TRUE LOVE NEVER DIES

It heightens
It brightens
It lights up your darkness
Your spirit it enlightens
It's in your war with you, it's roaming with its Vikings
It's hitting out of nowhere, slipping to you
It's spiking
It's lovingly frightening


Because, True Love Never Dies


For you it's always fighting


Because, True Love Never Dies


It's spiritually inclined
It will temporarily cause you grief whilst it somehow
  redefines
Its every move
To stand in line with your every line


Because, True Love Never Dies


It just modifies its position into your state of heart
  and sometimes that message takes a while to come
  through to your state of mind


It reignites
Itself somewhere for you
Every night
Sending you visions you may miss in your every sight
It sets a flight

 147

To your sparkling light
Presently present so disregard what you might

Because, True Love Never Dies

Oh, it's there all right

It repositions
Still keeping your heart as its prescription
Navigating through the galaxy of souls
Looking for the star with your name that's written

True love never dies because as much as the love belongs
   to you, you don't get to make that decision
It's present there,
It's something you don't need to envision
It's official, it's opinion and it stands there forgiven

Because, True Love Never Dies

It's forever living

So take a submarine
To your bloodstream
Let's take the route to the vessels upstream
Create a daydream from a dark street

Because, True Love Never Dies

Tell me,
You haven't felt it every time your heart beats

Even though sometimes you may feel like a prisoner
Where you cannot call a solicitor

Fighting against the minister
When the world's behaving sinister
And they look at you like an exhibitor
An unwelcome visitor
Taking the language of love right to the margins of
  the page
Really pushing the perimeter
Because it was your life you had to administer
And then accept the loss and sign it as heartbreak as
  the signature

But listen, true love never dies
It was never designated with a limiter

Because, True Love Never Dies

It becomes a symbol
That will now only occasionally sprinkle
Its love to you through the darkest moments,
Don't close your eyes,
Even if they're full of tears,
Let them fall,
You need them open,
Because something there in the darkness will twinkle

And it sets a tingle
That little tinkle
And to yourself you giggle
Because, True Love Never Dies

It will somehow send a signal

Spiritual
Make sure you're in a healthy state of heart so it can
  be reciprocal
Not everything you feel has to be visible
But the feeling alone can create the perfect visual

Because, True Love Never Dies

It's present in your life now,
Not living in your history
Not there for the drama
Not entertaining the bigotry
Making sure you have the greatest karma
And to the naked eye your glow is a mystery

Because, True Love Never Dies

As a love to begin with

Is the eternal victory

Because, True Love Never Dies
I'm telling you this, as that's what my mum said to me x

# DOES HEAVEN HAVE A BALCONY?

When I saw you there laying
Instantly I started praying
I didn't know what I was saying
I didn't know what price it would cost
But from that night I would forever be paying

I'd give my life for you to be here, staying
Bringing glory to the garden,
Elegance to the kitchen
A home full of love
Dance to the living room
Childhood memories of Action Man dolls, dinosaurs,
Making tents out of blankets, playing

I miss you so much
And every night I etch your name on the inside valve of
  my heart
Your smile
Your voice
I keep replaying

Wide awake insomnia laying
Feeling the weight of heartbreak that's sat on my chest
It's a heavy one
Down on me it's weighing
My broken light has grief displaying

A love lost conveying
A heart shattered but not appearing on my doctor's X-raying
And I wrote it in 'The White Rose'
And I will write it again
It still doesn't matter what they're saying

I miss you
Forgive me within these five years if there was ever a
  day I unintentionally dismissed you
I don't know if you remember us
I don't know if you think of us
I don't know if your heart broke just like mine
I don't know if you can throw me down some motherly love
Because all these lot are giving me is a big box of tissues
To wipe away my misery and anguish
But not aid for my internal issues

And I really wanna know if you were scared
When the angel of death picked you

And I really wanna know if you felt loved
When your final breath left you

And I really wanna know if you know how much I loved you
And I really wanna know if all of us was within you

And I really wanna know if your mum and dad came down
  from Heaven to help assist you
And I really wanna know if you miss us, the way we miss you

And no, I still haven't found the pot of gold at the end
  of the rainbow
And no, I still haven't found my guardian angel with its
  shining halo
And no, I still haven't found the tempo to my shadow
Or the ability to shoot my arrow through a path of pain
  that's night-time narrow
No James with a bond
No wizard with a wand
My life's been nicked,

I was thrown in a cage
60 seconds you were gone,
No harmony in a song
I never made it to space Mother,
But don't you worry, I kneel to the Lord
My arm's still strong
This is what my life's like,
This is my life's work,
I won't feel lifeless,
I'll fight for a lifeline,
To make my life long

No treasure in the sea
There are many missing pieces of me
To find peace in me
Is still a dream to be

There's no voice I want to hear
No similarity that comes near
There's no clarity, in the air
There's no sanity, when it flares
No comfort when it tears,
And most certainly no solidarity within the unit when
   you're not here
Funeral preparations
I became your project manager
A professional one
No way was I going to represent you as an amateur
The tears I saw from Grandmother
Distraught me into a mental massacre
Your birthday
The date you left
And every other important moment
Now hold a completely different calibre in our calendar

Your dresses still hang
Your perfumes still hold
The candles still smell of lavender

The stairs are hoovered
The fireplace still roars
The wooden parts are cleaned thoroughly on your
  beautiful banister

I'm still a single, eligible bachelor
I sat in your car for days when you left
Wishing for one more drive to be your passenger
There was a light around you Mother; I never got a
  chance to tell you
Your presence was a blessing and it was spectacular

You went in peace, you gracefully kept your sanity
Through all the drama, you kept firm with your gravity

But I do live anxiously, depression comes rapidly,
  randomly,
But I can handle it a lot better now, it's pretty decent
  the fact that I can handle it pretty casually

I refuse for your passing to be the reason I walk into
  insanity
PTSD will not keep me in the class as an examinee
I will find the capacity to control the calamity of this
  catastrophe
I find hope knowing you're in Heaven, that means when I,
  God willing, one day get there (IA)
There'll be great hospitality

I hope you're proud of me
When no one's looking, throw a white rose down if you can
If it lands in my lap
My theory will be true

Heaven does have a balcony.

# You Have A Granddaughter

We got the news the night you passed
Baji said you had a clue but even hearing that just hit
me hard I just sat there,
not knowing what to do,
I cried and laughed
How much of you is in this beautiful baby,
Even though she never will ever meet you
Nothing will ever set you two apart

# YOU MAY HAVE DIED BUT YOU ARE STILL ALIVE

Your name is my heartbeat
That pulses pure comfort to my pain
Your memory is more than a thought
That arrives to my aid
To shield me from insane

Your smile holds precision
As a perfect vision
One that solely holds the power to unite my emotional
  divisions

Your life I adorn
Your hug is warm
Your touch I mourn
Your promise I've sworn
And when your grief was born
Your light I've worn

Your voice I've found
Your prayers are now
Your teachings have become lessons in clouds
That surround my crown

Your name in my mind
My head I bow
And in our dreams, I'm glad it's me you found

The letters of your name
The smell of your clothes, make home
Your footsteps, show

# LIFE IS SAD & BEAUTIFUL

There's so much more we can cope
May your wings
Spread wide,
May your soul set flight
And just before we say goodbye
For you to rest in peace, power and paradise
I just really wanted you to know
You may have died
But you are still alive.

## Chapter Four

# DESTROYING

# DEPRESSION

*'Please mind the gap between the train and the platform.*
*This is a central line train to Ealing Broadway,'* is
what I would hear on the tannoys that rang through the
speakers of Redbridge station each morning as I would
embark on another mundane journey into Central London,
on a course that I had no idea why I was doing. I was in
my first year of university studying Quantity Surveying
at the University of Westminster. I remember selecting
this course around results day when I finished sixth
form. Everyone knew what they wanted to do; I wanted to
write poems for a living, but the biggest problem I had
was that I had no belief in myself - in my ability to go
ahead and do it.

There was nobody - and I mean absolutely nobody - in
my life I could look up to who had followed a career in
an unconventional manner in the creative arts. It was
just not a thing where I came from. I was always told
it was too hard and the odds were stacked up massively
against me. At some point after finishing sixth form and
going to university, I began believing that I was not
good enough to pursue a career in the creative arts. I
remember one time mentioning a particular school I wanted
to attend besides the sixth form I was at, but I was never
allowed to bring the prospectus home due to the distance
of the school. So I packed my pen and paper away and
began a course on the science behind making buildings.

This was the first step into a dark downhill spiral
of depression, which then led me to question why my
parents never let me move out. It was really a cultural
thing - that you only move out once you are married -
but I always wondered why my parents never let me. This
was another trigger as the three-year course went on; I
began failing modules, I had to resit, I lost the last
few remaining drops of passion I had and the Underground

became a place of reminding me that I had no dreams and certainly no ability within me to even believe that I did.

I didn't enjoy my university life at all and found myself spending more time looking at other people's experiences on social media. I began comparing my life to others. I then looked for reasons to not turn up. The only person I was fooling here was myself as it was me who was paying for the course. One day, I discovered that BBC Radio was right around the corner on Great Portland Street, and I began walking past it daily. The constant fanfare outside, the excitement, the production of the shows all seemed like a fascinating world, one that I had no business in besides walking past and hoping to catch a glimpse of it.

University was a real intense struggle - my lack of enthusiasm and care for the course showed in my lack of enthusiasm in group participation. Constantly hearing how '*university is meant to be the best time of your life*' and how '*you make friends for life there*' really built up my expectations for them not to be met at all. The comparisons, the 'why not me?' syndrome all led to my first real experience with depression. Little did I know that this encounter with the mental health struggle was a starter course for what was to follow instantly after my mother's passing.

Depression is one thing, but depression mixed with grief, loss, heartbreak and sudden death is a completely different ball game. I remember the night my mum passed, one of my friends who had also lost a parent came to me within the sea of people comforting me and said, 'This is the worst. It doesn't get any better for a long time, but if you can get through this, you can get through anything.' These words of brutal honesty hit me hard. I couldn't think of what a day on earth would look like

without my dear mother, let alone a lifetime of my time
left on earth.

I cried and cried and cried and cried so much that
I had no tears left. I became numb. I went for long
drives in my car by myself and I would scream so loudly
my voice would tremble. I'd seek comfort from wherever
I could find it. I was at my all-time lowest in life; I
was binge-eating junk food, I started smoking, which I
had never done in my life, and I started treating myself
like I was worthless.

I began getting up late; I had no concept of time -
each day was a blur. I had lost the fight, I had lost
the light; I was hopeless. There was nothing anyone
could say, nothing anyone could do that would move me.

I contemplated and entertained the thought of
suicide many times in my life and broke down various
times when explaining to some of my nearest and dearest
friends why I felt like I had to leave this earth.

I had nothing to live for.

I had nothing to get me up in the morning.

Nothing would make me laugh how I used to.

I felt as if my DNA was completely rewired after my
mum passed and I was a new, numb mess of a human.

But then something happened. One day something
really happened and it was something my mum's sister
said to me: 'your mum was able to survive without
her mum, so you can do the same without yours'. That
profound line hit me. It was then - in that moment
- that I realised I would not link depression to the
legacy of my mother; she did not deserve that. And
neither did I.

I started praying. I started drinking more water
and treating myself more kindly and allowing for the
spiritual signs of wherever my mum resided to find me

whilst I was in a respectable manner.

I remember one night so clearly: my mum visited me in my dream. I woke up crying and ran into my dad's room and told him, 'She's here; she's around and she came to see me.' He believed me and, from here, I started therapy. This was an experience in itself - it took three therapists before I found one I connected with in some aspect. I started running - 5ks, 10ks, 15ks, half marathons - I started eating healthier, I joined the gym, I implemented a routine ...

I wanted to change my life so I changed everything in my life.

And then in that moment truly realised that if you can make it out of your mind, you can make it anywhere.

Chapter Four was an incredibly dark phase, age and stage in my life, but it was in the darkness that I found gold dust; it was in the darkness that the brightest lights shone, and it was here in the darkness that I wrote the poems that helped me destroy depression once and for all.

Thank you for being with me this far. This one's a heavy one, but we can do it.

Let's destroy depression together ...

# THE PREGNANT MAN

You can't have expected me to tell you
When I didn't understand myself
But when you begin to fight the feelings
You start to fight yourself

I rally the troops,
As this war it sends no warning
And as I begin to face this battle
There is no one I could be calling

As time presses on, this tumour begins to grow
Transfixed to my inner body
It's not long at all now,
Until it's time for your show

I knew it from the start
You was there inside of me
As much as I would try to hide
Your darkness would brighten me

Compressed against our thoughts
This battle is underway
Going against everything I was taught
I will live to fight another day

Because, you can't have expected me to tell you
When I didn't understand myself
But when you begin to fight the feelings
You start to fight yourself

Then you kick in the night
And wake me up during my sleep
How can you be so impactful
For someone who can't be seen?

I hide you so well in front of others
Nobody has got any clue
But behind closed eyelids you come to life
And my heart you go straight through

You latch on to my feelings
Trap my inner health
Destroy any form of emotion
So you can have me to yourself
At first I didn't understand
And some days I still feel like I don't
But I've learnt if I don't speak on this matter it won't
  help
But the question is, do I want this problem to be
  solved?
You've come to show me you're all I have
So I only walk alone
You see that doesn't make sense
Because you are STUCK with me in my zone
And yes I can't change my words
But I can raise my tone
And yes I can't change my skin
But I can strengthen my bones
And yes I can no longer fly
But I can say that I have flown
And I will live to fight another day
Because I refuse to have you on my throne
So raise your body armour
As you walk through that door

Adapt the traits of your father
Pick yourself up from the floor
Prepare for war my little soldier
For you will take no more
As you learn the journey of a martyr
After all, it's true what they say: all is fair in love
   and war

You can't have expected me to tell you
When I didn't understand myself
But when you begin to fight the feelings
You start to fight yourself.

# SUBMARINE

How deep can we take it Captain?
If we ride along the tide our words may remain captive
So we begin to plunge and head towards the sea floor
And start to realise, vessels like us were not built to
  ride amongst the shore

As we begin to descend the more it is we discover
Firstly, the Indian and Atlantic were birthed from the
  same mother
Their waves slightly different yet similar to each other
And all attract visitors throughout the glorious summer

To capture the rumoured treasure buried in its unknown
  location
The preparation for depths. To be explored similar to a
  tourist destination
As the sea opens its waters with shared cooperation
At 2,000 feet under, we begin to see the ocean of
  purification

The land many may never see or ever visit
And a certain select few, may treat like a fairy tale
  gimmick
With only 5 per cent explored where man has been to
  exhibit
A tsunami may occur, but take a float with your spirit

As the navigation gains control,
Various spottings occur on the radar
We must tackle the one that's been growing inside
Captain, we're entering labour

Mayday Mayday is what the initial thought begins at
  sight
But looking at the other crew members, everything seems
  to be surprisingly all right
The propellers have now stopped, so be prepared to sail
  through with might
Let's open the doors and windows and brave how cold this
  water really is tonight


At 3,000 feet under, I begin to view everything as
  astrological
If actions speak louder than words, then surely this is
  illogical
As the circle gathers around I feel the warmth of this
  underwater oracle
And what happens next for my person will go down in my
  life as historical


I look to distract my thoughts, as my mind state becomes
  detrimental
Put on my life jacket and prepare to smash the windows
  of this submarine's temple
I begin to realise my childhood stories of mermaids and
  pirates were never once accidental
And now accept the fact that if I drown in my thoughts I
  pray for it to be gentle.

# THE DISTANCE

When I was feeling depressed
I was attached to my bed
I refused,
I wouldn't listen
To take in
Anything anyone said
Tired from sleeping,
But still I wanted more
Everything in my room, untidy
Belongings, are all over my drawers
My emotions unprocessed
Within my mind creating unneeded internal wars
But in order for me to achieve a great win
And to aid my psychological score
I had to overcome the biggest distance of the day
And that distance was between
My bed and the floor.

# I Can't Deal With All This Drama

I can't deal with all this drama
I don't know which way it folds
I can't deal with all this drama
This pain I can't but I need to let go

I can't deal with all this rain
You bring into my life
You got me questioning my sane
That can't be right?

I can't deal with all these conversations
With so much that was left unsaid
I can't deal with all these moments
From when we were at our best

I can't deal with all this drama
I don't know which way it folds
I can't deal with all this drama
This pain I can't but I need to let go.

# I WANT TO GO HOME

I want to live by your home-cooked food that speaks its
very own language to my body

I want to go home
On a land where you address my insecurities just as they
thought they found invisible places they could lobby

I want to go home
where my dreams meant something and didn't appear as
shallow halls

I want to go home
where light appeared where you were, no matter where my
shadow falls

I want to go home
but that's not possible

I want to go home
and I'm overwhelmed with sadness at the thought of that
not being probable

I want to go home
but home became a memory of the past

I instantly feel numb when I enter the graveyard,
We have no memories of being there together

I want to go home
I want to live how we lived, forever.

# SANDCASTLE

I build a sandcastle on the sand
A self-proclaimed king upon this golden land
Guarded by javelins and spears
Despite my fears, I still end up in no man's land,
But I still build a sandcastle on the sand.

# I Think I Need a Therapist

I think I need a therapist
To come and give me therapy
I think I need a therapist
I am worried, I am starting to believe everything I am
  telling me

I think I need a therapist
Someone to walk me through my mind
In the dark is where you'll find
All of me I hide

I think I need a therapist
Someone to guide me through these walls
I don't like the fact that I am starting to love this all

# ADDICTION

I thought I already told you you're not my best friend,
But here you are sitting in my silence as always,
Overstaying your welcome,
Mentoring me the wrong way,
Oh, me and you together used to be a quick thing,
But nowadays we're a long way
From where we once was
You take all my time
And I have given up pretending I don't know where all my
    time's gone, when we both know you have infiltrated my mind
Now you're running through my body
How can I be so on-point with you, but yet so off?
Numbing real love, and the tingling in the spine
You're not me
You're not real
You're not love
But why are you taking everything emotionally that's mine?
That's not OK, that's not fine
You're not us, addiction, you're not us
We're more than you
Our memories hold us together through tough times,
Like they say them tough people do
And even when you get me
I want you to know
You ain't getting through
I might not have a clue, but you haven't realised if
    that's the case
Then one day I might not have you
Because you might be all of me,
But I am not all of you
Hits heavy, addiction, cos you know it's true
You will not have me,
The day I will not have you.

# WASH YOUR FACE WITH TEARS

The world passes you by
As it falls from your eyes
As you wash your face with tears

Closure is far from near
Happiness isn't living round here
When you wash your face with tears

When your throat feels raptured
And your heart's not captured
When you wash your face with tears

Knowing there's no going back from here
And you don't get enough, because it's never enough from
  the ones who care
Your head pounds and your soul frowns
When you wash your face with tears

When goodbye holds no meaning
And the thought of a home, a home, is you dreaming
The sky cries
As the cloud hides
When you wash your face with tears

You turn the sound in the car higher
Because you're driving and screaming
Underwhelmed but overwhelmed through how much you're deeping
Not realising, unprocessed pain sits within you so long it's
  become a part of you and you're holding on and keeping
And nobody is seeing
How much your life is bleeding
When you wash your face with tears

Don't hold it back
Let it out
You take a deep breath in and then you scream and shout
Don't you ever give up,
Don't you ever entertain doubt
You're nowhere near knocked out
Just because you washed your face with tears

Now your eyes have dried
You lock and engage them with what love is to you
And you hold them tight
Because I promise you my friend,
It will all be all right
And if you want I'll sit with you through this one
I'm here,
This ain't my first rodeo
I'm proud to say I wash my face with tears.

# I Keep Punishing Me

The greatest times of my life when I should be
  flourishing
It's astonishing
Because I'm menacing my mind
And troubling my inner self
So as the world uplifts me in this moment of well-
  deserved glory
Myself, I am punishing
Externally smiling
Internally rummaging
For another excuse to hate myself
Another demon to entertain
Quickly hoping the greatness stops flourishing
Just so I can get back to the unprocessed pain that I
  must address in this moment of all to start publishing

I know I'm doing it
There's a huge acknowledgement
From my own establishment
Of my tolerance of ignorance
And self-punishment.

# VOICES

My mind's in a place where overthinking jumps into
  my sleep
Together they both dance to the sound of my heartbeat
They do something to me that I can't speak
This is something you feel, and the world can't teach

Depression has the power to hack nights
From dreaming and sleeping
Anxiety can snap ties
From friendships and feelings
You can feel a whole lot of pain
Without a whole lot of bleeding

The power of loss can hack nights and now there's no
  more sleeping
What makes it worse
Is when you hear voices
And there's no one speaking.

# MUM, MAN

I've moved out Mum, now I miss you even more
It runs deeper in a new property you've never seen
I never thought it could have got worse from your
  special kitchen drawer
There's so much that has happened Mum, I wanna know if
  it's all of us you saw
Did you see the weddings,
Do you see us push and carry on
Did you know it's been really hard
Did you think I was able to hang on?

I'm proud of myself Mum,
I hope you feel the same
I know I haven't done things the way the tradition would
  have wanted me to,
But I promise I will one day

I gave up everything for my art Mum,
I hope that's OK
I know we didn't discuss whatever happens if things go
  this way
But I'm OK Mum,
I behave like we're all OK
Could I have done more?
Should I have done more?
What do you think I'm thinking about? When I'm walking
  out the door?

That we couldn't have sunk more
Couldn't love more
Couldn't bring myself to bring you near me
Could I have stopped wars?

Could've moved back
Could've changed facts
Could've switched gears,
Could've worn hats
Could've brought back
The nights of darkness and pitch black
Could've done this, could've broke traps
Could've done that, when I shouldn't have loved back

Should I have done more?
What do you think I'm thinking about? When I'm walking
  out the door?

That we couldn't have sunk more
Couldn't love more
Couldn't bring myself to bring you near me
Could I have stopped wars?

# ᴅISAPPOINTED

I know you're disappointed
I can feel it
You don't need to be in the same universe to have it
  made clear to me
Your spirit is forever in my number one position
  appointed

But I completely get it,
I am too,
I'm more than disappointed

I swear we tried our best to make sure it was all
  avoided
I can't bear to see you one day and attempt to say, 'but
  wait, look, my point is'
Because your legacy is disjointed

Therefore, it's completely valid, that you're
  disappointed

Please forgive me,
I can feel you're disappointed.

# ᴅʀɪᴠɪɴɢ ᴘᴀsᴛ

You're still standing strong
Double-glazed and double-fronted
Through the countless nights of drama you've endured
And the trauma you've confronted

I can't bring myself to look you in your face
As I'm driving past
But I go out of my way to
Cross our paths
Because I still want you to know
You live so deeply in my broken heart

I will never have what I have with you on another dance
Nor will I ever feel what I felt in you
It doesn't matter if I spend the rest of my aching life
Trying to find a fighting chance

You were my Heaven on earth
You were my favourite art

Now the best we have
Is me catching a glimpse of you from the corner of my eye
As I'm driving past

I'm so proud of you, that you're still standing strong
Double-glazed and double-fronted
Through the countless nights of drama you've endured
And the trauma you've confronted

I can't bring myself to look you in your face
As I'm driving past
But I go out of my way to

Cross our paths
Because I still want you to know
You live so deeply in my broken heart.

# Kumbaya / Come By Here

My mum always used to say,
*People will come to see you three times in your life:*
*When you're born*
*When you get married,*
*And when you die.*

It's meant to go in that order
But my generation crossed the page,
Pushed the margin
Dismantled and broke the border
Now the spectrum's broader, but the life span's shorter,
Kumbaya, my Lord, kumbaya
I'm praying for the mental health disorder

He was 17, a bedroom-messy, sloppy teen
Eating a full English breakfast at quarter past three
On a hot summer's day would come home with muddy knees,
On them hard-to-wash denim jeans,
He'd say, 'Mum, I'm going to see the world and take you
   with me
'Because Dad wasn't here I'm going to give you
   everything you gave me'
He used to kiss my cheek every time right there
And his football boots were a bloody nightmare
But he was my nightmare, he was my dream
He was our lad, he was my Dean

Kumbaya, my Lord, kumbaya
My son is internally screaming my Lord, come by here
My son is psychologically bleeding my Lord, come by here
My son is planning on leaving me my Lord, come by here

Mine, kissed me too
Right above my cheek
And every morning would say, 'Mum make sure your
  eyebrows are on fleek'
He'd never wear a shirt unless it was ironed
His grades in school were good, for his dad he kept trying
He liked his protein shakes with dreams to play for West
  Ham
Then as he grew older he'd say, 'Mum I've got facial
  hair, see me, I'm a big man'
No mum should bury her son and no grandson should be
  buried by his nan

Kumbaya, my Lord, kumbaya
My son is internally screaming my Lord, come by here
My son is psychologically bleeding my Lord, come by here
My son is planning on leaving me my Lord, come by here

He never liked cricket, mine, he liked Indian tea and
  biscuits
And hated driving next to big lorries; he'd never risk it,
If you asked him to get something from the car he'd put
  on the closest pair of shoes, normally my heels and
  give us all a right show
Annoying, he used to block the sink with hairs from his
  comb
Walk around the house with his flashy bathrobe
He even did the mehndi dance at his sister's wedding and
  now his little baby nephew will never know
That his uncle went to university and never came home
I'm the mum I should've known

Kumbaya, my Lord, kumbaya
My son is internally screaming my Lord, come by here
My son is psychologically bleeding my Lord, come by here
My son is planning on leaving me my Lord, come by here

They say mums know it all
But we clearly don't
If I knew what he was fighting
Son: 'What could you have given me Mum?'
Mum: 'I could have given you hope
'I wouldn't have let this thing change you
'As your mum you should have given me that one more
  chance to save you
'I would never have betrayed you
'I carried you, I brought you here,
'Why wouldn't you let me even try to save you?'

Sons:
*I didn't mean to take your youth when I hatched from you*
*I didn't mean to break your heart and give it back to you*
*I didn't mean to take your soul and watch it detach from you*
*I didn't mean to, but I would do anything to come back*
  *to you*

*We have made our mothers cry my Lord*
*Kumbaya*
*We still fight the fight my Lord*
*Kumbaya*
*We will lay down our ego my Lord*
*Kumbaya*
*For the love of our mothers my Lord*
*Kumbaya*
*We shall walk as one my Lord*
*Kumbaya.*

# Mother Tongue

I went to war without recruiting an army
Stared at my enemy with two feet strong
I stood on the frontline and thought nothing could harm me
And that is where I went wrong

This pitch-black war zone sends no warning
Soldier, the enemy is approaching and it will last till
  morning
I awake from my sleep to prepare for my calling
I have seen it before, when the midnight is falling

When you hear them sirens you create your ammo
My thoughts become pelicans so I intertwine them to my
  arrows
This call of duty led my black ops down a path that's
  narrow
Behold, the black pearl was not only discovered by
  Captain Jack Sparrow

Lone soldiers cannot sail through the night
After hours these waters are forbidden
The ocean, you don't know her, she isn't nice
She covers your enemies as they are swimming hidden

By yourself you can try hard
Many before us have tried to swim alone and never made
  it back to the boatyard
Trust me,
You cannot fight a tsunami without a lifeguard

My Sergeant told me,
Be honest
Or how else would we connect?
Honest, he said
A word I am still to understand yet

Back to ground, I return to rally the troops
The strongest fighter from the land, the queen of the
  castle I approached her roof
Never lost a battle, never shed a tear,
Never thought twice on a decision, and showed purity
  beats fear

I request for her to join me, but this request lies
  deeper,
Her name is my mother, and up until now she never knew
  this battle existed either,

I went to war without recruiting an army
Stared at my enemy with two feet strong
I stood on the frontline and thought nothing could harm me
And that is where I went wrong

Mum, it's me,
I have been fighting demons at night in my sleep
Mum, it's me,
I have covered my lies through the smiles of my teeth
Mum, it's me

I have fought this battle for far too long
I have tried to stop the way I am feeling
I have sat and cried to the words of every slow song
I even have my own guardians of the galaxies to fight my
  midnight demons

Man down, man down Sergeant
Suicide has taken our soldier
Man down, man down Sergeant
Who did it get this time? It took bipolar
Man down, man down Sergeant
If you can hear me the war is not over
I repeat, if you can hear me the war is not over
Peace of mind, it makes no sense to die for it
Your war zone will lead you to victory, but you, my
  soldiers, will have to fight for it

So don't you dare give in,
Don't you dare throw in the towel,
If it's knocked you down again and again, get back up
  because together we are going one more round

Your story doesn't end here
It's only a chapter that has finished
Welcome to Act 2 Scene 1
And we have some brand-new characters in it

First, honesty
Second, trust
Third, companionship
Fourth, must

When you drop your guard, depression will flood in
And anxiety isn't going to knock, she will let herself in
And in that moment when the world can seem so cruel
They will call you a little mummy's boy, but tell them,
  Mama didn't raise no fool

Feel no shame or guilt in what you feel
For many around you encounter the same battle, just on a

different playing field
I take my sleeping tablets and antidepressants and fling
   them out of this window
They will no longer detach my mind and thoughts each
   night making me a midnight widow

I refuse to let it define me
I refuse to let it beat me
I refuse to have another sleepless night
Because of what lies beneath me

Yes, I went to war without recruiting an army
Yes, I stared at my enemy with two feet strong
Yes, I stood on the frontline as if nothing could harm me
And you know what my mum said, 'Son you was never wrong.'

# WHAT TRIGGERED HIM?

We need to know this
In order to decipher the situation
If we can't figure out what triggered him
We can't come to a healthy realisation

I get it
He's acting irrational
I need you to calm down
You screaming and shouting
Is making this episode about all of you
Sorry to break it to you
It's not about all of you right now

What happened son?
Did you hear a song that upset you?
A moment in a movie really get you?
Or was it a thought that interrupted your thinking and
    now you're back to a place where all little things
    affect you?

He's not speaking much to his friends
His family have no hope in Heaven
We need to install a disciplined routine
Firstly make sure he's in bed without his phone by 11

It's hard to say what's affecting him
And unless he's willing to speak
We can't really get him help
Because it's his word not ours
And it's deep
I'm going to go now
I'll make sure to come back first thing

But I just want you to know son,
You're going to be more than fine

All of us are willing to do everything.

# TELL THEM

Tell them it took my heart
About a hundred thousand times
Tell them I don't know what to do
Like 99 per cent of the time
Tell them I don't like to sleep
And I hate the words 'good night'

Tell them I cry to my Lord
Tell them my heart doesn't get bored
Tell them it's just another night for me to turn these
  words into chords
Tell them my soul is made of stone and I can't pull the
  sword

But tell them we made it through the wire
Tell them the world will know about the stories of the
  boys from the shire
On how it took me time to climb the wire
And this little rain doesn't help in a world full of fire

Tell them I'm not leaving
Tell them I'm still breathing
Tell them I'm scared
Of everything I'm not achieving.

# It's in the Interests of the Devil for Me to Give Up

My thoughts are running wild, I'm wondering why
Every night I'm stuck in this tug of war
Most times I don't even know what I'm fighting for
Trying to get it, the bigger picture
Living through a devil's dreams for the Holy Scripture

I sit there crying until the morning, like I'm mourning
For a life I've never lived, I've had so many warnings
A life that's never boring, shots but never scoring
I overdosed on pills one night, and still woke up in
  the morning

Mum's clocking on, I'm just trying to please her
God's speaking to me when I look at baby E
Telling me, 'Mammo, come on stay strong, you can do
  this'
It's my mind baby boy, sometimes I feel like I'm going
  to lose it.

# TAKE THREE

Surviving these episodes
Should come with a medal
The same as trying to navigate through mental hell with
  no chain, gears, directions or pedals
Thinking you're the answer
And eventually everything will settle
Look, I'm very well aware I can fight to get through this,
But I don't want to get to another level
With extra voices and added treble
I'm being honest
I'm not being mental
But I'm not sure how many heartbreaks one man can
  survive
Let alone live through several
I won't do it
But I do think of it
I haven't written about you in a while
But now I'm in the thick of it
The only way I'm dying is from natural causes
I promised myself, Mum, and the ones I love,
And that's how I'll live through it.

# FOR I AM JUST A MAN

*Us men need to do a better job of checking each other*
*- that's checking in, but also checking behaviour*
*that's toxic.*

Who moves when his desire calls
Or attempts to address it when it stands against him tall?
Where in front of hardly anyone I lower my guard
Or open my arms
And purposefully miss the ship that delves deep to
  my heart
For I am just a man
Who maintains his facade of looking hard

For I am just a man
Who wouldn't dare truly speak his mind
Uncomfortably comfortable living between the rhymes,
In a time of the lines
Breaking rules, overstaying my bedtime
To get lost in the psychological state of the night-time
For I am just a man
Who never listens to the whistle that's blown in overtime

For I am just a man
Governed by his desire
Constantly holding on to faith whilst attempting to
  navigate as closely away as I can from the fire
I am just a man who overthinks all of this, but would
  never speak because I am just a man who would never
  retire

For I am just a man
Who doesn't acknowledge potential
I don't really ever do what I can
For I am just a man
Who doesn't know who I am

For I Am Just A Man x

# 1 Cannot Let You Love Me

Even though you see me sensitive
Take it upon yourself to become my emotional executive
I cannot let you love me

Even though we're completely different
That's what makes us miraculously, magically magnificent
I cannot let you love me

Even though you know exactly how to handle me when I am
  impulsive and impatient
Though our parallel lives that were never meant to cross
  are now doing so, tenderly adjacent
I cannot let you love me

Even though your touch is vulnerable, firm and soft
I am not willing to pay what it costs
I cannot let you love me

I'd rather a dagger every time through my art,
When I see you happy inside the life of another heart
Because I cannot and I will not let you love me

You were the closest out of them all,
But I'm so sorry, I cannot let you in,
I cannot let you love me.

# DEPRESSION IN PERSON

I've turned off the lights
I've closed the curtains
Kissing my teeth as loud as I can
Because I know for certain
The moment I shut my eyelids my night worsens
Because that's when there's no escaping
Depression in person
Heavy innit
The weight of your own human burden?
Exhausted and then overthinkings bursting
Mum was right
I never learn
It's not a surprise even now at my big age I'm still not
   learning
But I feel like every night I'm just rehearsing
What it feels like to be a better version
I don't know if it's working
Not all of these self-harm scars
Some are survival marks
I was bitten by a couple of serpents
So yeah meeting new people makes me nervous
Even when I know my purpose
I just don't want there to be anything ugly about you or
   me above or beneath the surface
I've turned off the lights
I've closed the curtains
Kissing my teeth as loud as I can
Because I know for certain
The moment I shut my eyelids my night worsens
Because that's when there's no escaping
Depression in person.

# No, No, No

What are you doing?
Why are you slipping back to your self-destructive
  mannerisms so speedily?
You've been through worse
You've become much better at handling hurt
Don't do this to yourself,
Don't fast-track your pain so easily

Don't exaggerate it
Allow yourself the decency
To return back to your frequency.

# ⁊ Mustn't

I mustn't allow you to consume all of my head
As you already occupy the main state of my heart
I mustn't distance myself more than I already have from
the world
And behave as if it was the world that pushed me and
others further apart

I mustn't wrestle my demons untrained
Or dance with the devil unchained
I mustn't let the post-trauma dominate my brain and trip
me up at the start
I mustn't entertain these bad habits
For they'll just tie their bonds stronger with grief

I mustn't be attached to a device like a drip in the
night, as it will most certainly happily steal all of
my sleep
I mustn't be too hard on me
As this doesn't lead to my peace
I mustn't do what I mustn't do
But I must always love me.

# Sometimes I Feel Like Crying

Sometimes I feel like crying
Because the pain is unbearable
Sometimes I feel like crying
Because certain words cause mental damage that is not
  repairable
Sometimes you're the only one feeling what you're
  feeling around all the people you love
So nobody understands because, truth is,
What you are going through
Is not comparable

I'm still yet to receive the dialysis
The answers of the analysis
Of the multiple times I've not been able to grow through
  multiple problems
I've lost all movement in a panic episode of my
  psychotic paralysis

PTSD every time I see an ambulance
Now I've got more bars than my nephew's abacus
Pages full of pain
Dancing with suicide as the lead character, that's the
  savageness

The desire the scandalous
The plants the cannabis
The tightrope the balances
The antagonist the catalyst
The agendas and the accidents

An education system that is designed to make you feel
  inadequate

Playing dress up as a graduate
But now I'm not being aggressive,
I'm just being adamant
Because if you want real change, that means someone's
  losing their seat from the senior leadership team
  management
Because an ethnic minority is the new inhabitant
Oh, add a little more masala to make the entrance
  extravagant
The ultimate postgraduate
Only know how to do things one way,
When we take it to the maximum

Good intentions versus malicious intent
Real clean hearts lost in a matrix designed for us to
  fail, but would rather die than keep it any less than
  100 per cent
I'm content to the fact that it's art, it's not content
The only time you hear that word around here is at the
  front of the book at the contents
Because these pages are not designed for algorithms,
But they hail from the home where there are hundreds of
  shoes in porches covered in smoke from the aroma of
  agarbatti incenses
Humour and suspense
Where you know it and you are not perfect
But you're down to reflect

Sometimes I feel like crying
Because the pain is unbearable
Sometimes I feel like crying
Because certain words cause mental damage that is not
  repairable
Sometimes you're the only one feeling what you're

feeling around all the people you love
So nobody understands because, truth is,
What you are going through
Is not comparable

I'd rather a spiritual prescription than a virtual
  subscription
I'd prefer one true friend, than a fake world that
  doesn't listen
I'll fight for a better right for justice for those
  in prison
The story is all about the white rose,
But I never really wrote about the dirt from which it
  had risen
Mazes and prisms
Every heartbeat it is hitting
But I always listen to Mum, even now she's not here,
  I hear her as loud as ever

She'd say
'It doesn't matter, it's already written'

Sometimes I feel like crying
Because the pain is unbearable
Sometimes I feel like crying

Because certain words cause mental damage that is not
  repairable
Sometimes you're the only one feeling what you're
  feeling around all the people you love
So nobody understands because, truth is,
What you are going through
Is not comparable.

# Social Emotional Battery

There are not many places I can charge this
There are no sockets in the walls
Or plugs with pins
Definitely no electric points in car parks to spark this
Not many places to charge my social emotional battery to
  give me everything.

# Because You Understand Survival

After reviewing the emotional analysis,
You have to live where the magic and tragic is,
In order to become the protagonist
And then you'll realise,
Being brave was always part of the narrative.

# TEARS IN JARS

Would you keep my tears in jars?
Would you unpack their process or would you push them
    far?
Would you see them as fallen planets or see them as
    falling stars?
Would you see my tears as mine or would you see my tears
    as ours?

Would you keep my tears in jars?
Would you keep my fears in your vehicle and not tell me
    if you're switching cars?
Would you read along to what I write, as I write our
    memoirs
or would you see me as broken and unfixable, just a good
    attempt of a healing scar?

Would you keep my tears in jars?
Would you keep them close to your present and past?
Would you let them flow through your artery and
    influence your heart?
Would you give me a head start; if you was to present
    bad news do I get a jump-start, a fresh start, when my
    heart's taken all your dead parts
or do I just share my pain with the world and witness
    its growth in algorithms and bar charts?

Would you keep my tears in jars
or would you leave them in a world that's ours?

Would you keep my tears in jars?

# YOU GOT YOURSELF

I don't know what my older sister would tell my niece
But I know on her shoulder my baby niece would cry
I don't know what my older sister would tell my nephew
But I know that little soldier will keep asking her why

I don't know who would say I just gave up
I don't know who should respect my honour and say 'na,
   trust me, he tried'
I don't know if anyone would sit up and pray for me nightly
I don't know who would keep my name alive

I don't know why I think these things
I don't know why I punish myself inside my mind
I don't know why nobody's word is ever enough
I don't know why I look for things, I don't know I'm
   looking for, hoping it will make things all right

I don't know why I worked so hard on myself
For me to be back here thinking what it would be like to
   finally escape the night
I don't know me, I don't know you, I don't know I,
I don't know purpose; when I'm like this, I don't know
   reason, I don't know mine

I don't know how to cope with my thoughts and their
   mechanics
I don't know how to accept that the world is corrupt
   and that I want kids, but don't want to bring kids
   into this planet that's designed institutionally with
   barbaric dynamics
I don't know how we overlook people being massacred,
   tortured and killed and then say the biggest

conversation is plastic
I don't know how the nations are not united and the game
    of politics has become a pure game of theatrics and
    dramatics
I don't know how to laugh; I never got into slapsticks

I don't know how you break an episode, mental torture
    within a cycle
I don't know why I know where to walk on the steps
    within the darkness of my spiral
I don't know why I stretch my tears to fall over the
    midnight mile
I don't know why I recover and heal, but then self-
    destruct in my overthinking brain when I put myself on
    trial
I don't know why I lie, when I don't know why I smile

I don't know where I find hope
But I just somehow do
I don't know how I create love
When I really don't have a clue
I don't know why I keep going
I guess I never will
I don't know why I let bad thoughts overtake the good
    ones,
When the good ones are great and just equally real
I don't know why I'm so consumed by the way I feel
I don't know much, clearly,
But I do know the deal
I do know fight,
I do know the drills
I do know triggers
I do know the skills
I do know art saved my life

I do know poetry was my pill
I don't know you,
But I know you will,
I wish you well
Keep in touch with yourself and congratulate yourself on
  how far you've come
Please do tell
Because dealing with your thoughts alone is like walking
  with one fire extinguisher
Right through hell
So give someone a bell
Sit and cry, laugh and gel,
You ain't alone,
What the hell am I doing up here if you are?
Don't get me started on you as well
Essentially
Take care of yourself mentally
Carefully
Restfully
Pleasantly
Medically
You don't need to fight yourself anymore
You are not your own enemy
Now sensibly
Splendidly
Welcome help
That doesn't make you seem helplessly
Recovery
Tremendously
Healing successfully
Living respectively
In your own skin
Acceptably
I don't know much

But I know we will get there steadily
You have so much to live for,
You have your entire legacy
I don't know but I also know I don't
Need to punish, myself
Or I won't flourish, my health,
Yourself won't publish yourself
Now come on, breathe with me, let's carry it well,

I got you,
But most importantly
You got yourself.

# SOMETIMES

Sometimes a search engine can't find the answer you're
    looking for
And no friend can string together the words on the end
    of a phone
Sometimes you can get lost so deep into your own mind
You can be smiling and laughing in a car with your
    friends, but literally be driving alone

Sometimes the nights are painful to sleep through
So you stay awake and try to fight
But you end up getting knocked out before midnight and
    lie there and cry

Sometimes you draft messages to post online
Read them back to yourself and delete them because it's
    borderline attention-seeking
Borderline screaming for help because you're not fine

Sometimes you still put others first when you're
    defeated because you don't know yourself well enough
    to know how to be kind

Sometimes a book can't turn to a page that gives you the
    answers you require
Sometimes the touch from the warmest lover of lust
    can't give you the feeling you thought your inner self
    needed and desired
Sometimes you forget to thank yourself for how far you
    have come, even at times when there was nothing in the
    world for you that was inspired
Sometimes you forget people love you
No they really do

Sometimes you let your overthinking get in the way and
  influence all of you
Sometimes you don't realise how powerful and capable you
  are
Sometimes you think it's over, but that's not a decision
  you get to choose
And the most important one of them all
Is sometimes you forget to say to yourself

I Love You x

# A Little Bit of Empathy

I'm extremely sensitive and empathic
Which means whatever is or isn't projected
Unknowingly, knowingly, I wear it

I'm forever training my mind to be at a gold medal
    equivalent of being emotionally athletic
Because as much as I try, if I feel it, I feel it;
    I can't reject it
It's internally externally invisibly magnetic

I can't speak to everyone about this
Some people think I'm being pathetic and they give me
    that vibe of being apathetic

I tried reading books
I really tried understanding this from a point of view
    that's theoretic
But before I know it, I've sunken back into it and I'm
    here feeling too many feelings, now feeling to be
    apologetic

Hence why I decided to write another poetic paragraph
Before calling a poetic paramedic
Because sometimes it's disastrous and other times it's
    epic

Empath to empath
Chest to chest
Art to art
Heart to heart
You realise it quick
There's something in the aura of the empathic aesthetic

I wish I could take off emotions that aren't mine, it's
affecting my psychological score of credit, do you get
me, do you get it?

# Best Friend

You always know what to say
I don't even need to speak
You make me think what I did was wrong,
Without patronising or shouting when you're telling me

You lift my frown when it carries weight
You check into my multiple dimensions and sometimes it
  gets very late
And all I can really say is

I don't know where I'd be without you mate

When I'm better I'll be able to help
Because I know you're going through some stuff too,
And like you say, 'talking about your problems is good
  for your health'
So link up innit, let's do some more talking boo

You still annoy me much,
Don't get excited
But sometimes it's important I tell you,
I love you best friend,
I don't know where I'd be without you x

# I Am My Mother's Son

You haven't won
Your demons done
You've lost me
To me you're scum
It's good you are far away
So far it's taken me the distance to realise,
I am my mother's son

Your energy was never the one
My mind you spun
With your artificial fun
I watched you run
Carrying the weakest ton
You wouldn't stand a chance in this one-on-one
I'm not just anyone

Her prayers extend far beyond the grave

For your own interest, please don't you ever forget

I Am My Mother's Son.

# I Promise You, It Becomes More Manageable

From when it seems impossible to continue
One morning you will waken and discover it has become
more manageable

I didn't say easier,
I didn't say it disappears
But you do learn to develop coping mechanisms
From the nights where your own thoughts
Are unimaginable

I PROMISE YOU

You will smile again
Your spirit will feel light again
You will get another chance at life again

Because I promise you,
It becomes more manageable.

## Chapter Five

# THE BEAUTY AND THE PEACE

Finding peace after grief became one of the most challenging necessities I had to achieve in order to reclaim some form of sanity within my life. Losing my mother unfortunately came with no warning signs; it came with no coping manuals, mechanisms, guidebooks or teachings. She did, however, repeat a particular saying which helped me massively. My mother lost her father when she was very young and her dear mother a little while after, and with these two heartbreaking losses in her life, she kept repeating to us as children:

'When I die, I want you to cry and get over it.'

I never understood the value of these words at the time, as when you hear them from your mother you are truly ignorant enough to believe that she will be alive forever. Unfortunately, that is not the reality of the matter.

My mother's death is definitely the rawest pain I have ever felt. It drove me to the edges of life; it took me to the darkest of places within my mind. And led me to many times in my life when I did not want to be alive anymore. However, when going through these mental distresses, panic attacks, traumas and stages of grief, a variety of things came to my aid to help me through the slow minutes of each day, the sadness of witnessing other families together as a family and the forever Mother's Day marketing material produced by companies.

The first thing that really helped carry me through was true friendship. My mum would say a lot of the time:

'You will realise who is there for you,
when I am not here.'

Again, another gem full of wisdom that I was unable to relate to at the time due to not having experienced a loss so significant. But she was right - many people came but only a handful stayed. At this point I had gone through such turbulence with my working career; everything was really everywhere. But true friendship looks past who your achievements make you out to be; true friendship is the friendship of the connection of souls, light, darkness and love. It's the ability to sit in the darkness with someone you love, allowing them to honour the emotions but not overstay their welcome in a toxic environment. True friendship for me transformed into being a shoulder or knee to cry on, hands to lift me from the floor as I lay screaming in agony; it became sleepovers, checking in; it became long drives in the car with nowhere to go, conversations that were deep and heavy; and at times, looking back now, I feel in that period of my life when my dear mother passed, the friendships that helped carry me through that tragic time really did become family. To all my friends who walked with me in my grief, I thank you.

Besides friendship, art was a significant tool that I used to really engage my mind, especially when I started punishing myself when there wasn't anybody to phone, because these moments do come too. It became a calling card, a special bond - it was as if poetry was reinvented to me for the very first time. It became something sacred and it really and truly did become a lifeline.

The pieces you read earlier in the book - 'The White Rose', 'If She Was Here', 'The Best Years' - are just some of the poems that poured out of my heart, and I sat crying relentlessly whilst writing them.

Art became a component I could not live without. It

set a fire in my soul - one that I have come to realise I must protect and respect at all times.

Another major component that was installed in my life from the moment my mum passed was prayer. I did pray a fair bit whilst she was here, but truthfully speaking, I was disconnected and not as heavily involved as I became after she passed. Strengthening my relationship with my Lord, manifesting the ability to pray, gave me a purpose I am truly grateful for.

Thank you for being with me on this journey so far. We have approached the final stage of *Life Is Sad and Beautiful*. I wish you well on your journeys of love, life and grief, and I could not be prouder to present the final chapter:

The Beauty and the Peace.

# HOME

It's warm
It's cuddly
It's full of love and care
It's the right temperature
It's the right atmosphere
Happiness is always somewhere near

You sleep well
Your hearts gel
You hold each other's fears

It's not a postcode
Or a zip code
It's just somewhere inside here

You're not anxious or paranoid
You're not overwhelmed and annoyed
Because you control what happens here

Home,
Take me there,
Where I can be free of my demons
I can love without reason
I can stay clear of those who stay schemin'
I feel no PTSD
I am no longer silently screaming
I enjoy the seasons
I fix all my broken pieces
I understand family for its entirety and its true
  meaning

Where you're awake but it feels like you're dreaming

Home

When you walk through the door, it's one loving feeling.

# CLASS OF COVID-19

Well, what a journey we've had
Friendships have fallen together and fallen apart, but
   if they're meant to be in your story they'll boomerang
   back
We lost loved ones, now we have them in our hearts and
   dreams; they wouldn't want us to be sad
Isolated in isolation really brought out some pretty
   good things in some of us; for some of us, let's be
   real, it was pretty bad
But that's OK, it's OK to recognise
But it's not OK to be not OK and to let that be the only
   feeling you have
Answer the phone when your mum calls you,
Let that be your launch pad
I know it can be really hard, but sometimes make that
   extra effort with your dad
We're outspoken as ever, but still have to hold our
   tongues in certain moments because when someone can't
   hold the conversation, they want to hold the room and
   make it mad
Grandma outlived everyone in her generation, and I can
   see it from her face she would do anything for one
   more conversation with Grandad
We survived, you're alive, practise gratitude and, even
   if it's for a moment, try to be glad
Salute to the ones who became allies and real ride-or-
   die comrades
Because class,
This year was full of chaos
And nobody blew the whistle
We all had to play to play on

Even when we were injured, and through moments that were
    hard to process because the government's behaviour was
    fickle
There's not been a moment for a substitution
We're witnessing drama daily, it's as if we're alive in
    an episode of *Jerry Springer*
You got to stay on and fight through all of your
    overthinking nightmares and delicate divisions
Switched on
Smartphone users
Being fed fake news with online rumours
Virtual movers
Being viewed by millions of viewers
Ah, our generation got lost
But it found itself at the same time
That's why we're full of big mouths
Addressing everything that's been under the carpet
Not really here to play by the rules of 'hold on, this
    conversation might just take some time'
Don't let anyone,
Especially anyone toxic, get too close to your heart
    and mind
I don't care if you think you're fine
You let them too close
They'll creep their way in and discover things you never
    really wanted them to find
So to say no, is absolutely fine
Fitness became a universe within a universe
Beauty set new boundaries
Online shopping just became the thing
Now my fingers click on things, and my brain is thinking
    'ah look what found me'
YouTube I'm lost in for days
Everything's now recommended for me

That's why I'm flicking through videos of justice being
  served and anything else that is really worthy of me
I don't know about you
But this year felt like a burden to me
Listen, don't worry
You're going to have that dream wedding
And you will just celebrate your birthday late
If it continues, we just got to focus on what we can
  control and move with love never haste
What I've learnt
If you can control your mind when it doesn't seem
  allowable
You graduate the class
You become mentally powerful.

# Cultural Identity Crisis

Poetry by nature
Of course I represent Ammi Jaan and Papa
It was 1960 when they left Azad Kashmir, in my DNA I
  have the ability, capability, agility, the hustle, of
  my Beji and Baba

I come from homes of agarbatti incense and hands where
  your kismet
Can't be read because they're covered in Elephant Atta

I represent my heritage
My sister's
My mother's
Grandmother's
Father's
My brother's
Grandfather's
And my baby kakka's

I come from the heat of the tandoor and the smell of
  sehri paratha

I represent mountainous Azad Kashmir
Every Pakistani whose name was never pronounced
  correctly
And every one of us who never got to live their dream
You are so much more whilst being a Hala and Chacha

I represent the hairiest arms
The thickest eyebrows
The extravagant walimas
The tabla sounds

I am Kashmiri
I am proud.

# THE BEST OF THE LAST

We'd knock on each other's front door to ask our
  friend's parents if they were allowed to play outside
Now we wait for icons to appear besides our usernames to
  show each other that we are online

We'd support local businesses by buying necessities from
  small, privately owned shops
Now we click and collect or select 'express', just to
  make sure our parcel isn't delayed or forgot

We'd cherish the ability of capturing authentic magical
  moments on film
Now we modify, edit, alter the image and its filtered
  components; now the debate is what part of the image
  is real

We'd have our working-class pockets full of change made
  of zinc, copper and nickel
Now it's virtual currency, immediate gratification and
  showing off to belittle

We'd all pitch in, in tradition to ensure the smell of
  what's cooking fills the entire home from the kitchen
Now we sit in one position, click to order 'recently
  had' on repetition, not caring for the process of time
  curated in nutrition

We'd take the battery out of the Tamagotchi the moment
  it died to help it have another chance of life
Now we unfollow and immediately despise our people for
  not instantly appreciating our latest post believing
  it was haste as the reason they didn't like

We'd spend hours selecting the right font on clip art
We'd have keyrings that were torches to help us through
  the night when it got dark
We'd be on teletext checking the weather
We'd get a bucket and spade and dig in the garden to
  find buried treasure
We'd close our eyes and try to recite things we'd
  memorised from the textbook to show family members
  'Wait, hold on, I'm actually clever'

We'd find reasons to play in the rain whenever
We'd have one-on-ones then shake hands to sort the
  matter wherever

When we'd be in a room,
We'd be in the room together.

# The Good Old Days

I was knocking on the front door
You wouldn't have to call me
The TV in black and white
The radio did everything for me
Me and you my love
The internet never saw me
We are here to light it up
Let me tell my story

We come from a generation
We sacrificed, made love
We grew through situations
That meant we're never giving up

But somehow it's all wrong
Now that the love is gone
I don't know if I'm the only one who wants to sing this song

Can you take me back to the good old days?
To the good old days
To the good old days

You better run up the stairs fast
Or the monster will come and get you
When you lost a tooth
You better pray the fairy don't forget you
To go out late
Never would they let you
But you did it anyway
The rules would never set you
Now they say the thing to do is to 'take photos of
  your food'

Now I'm not being rude
But your generation hasn't got a clue
So I hold on to how I live
These traditions, they're not new
But can someone please take me back to the good old days
So I can feel brand new?

Can you take me back to the good old days?
To the good old days
To the good old days.

# MIDNIGHT GRIEF CLUB

As the clock strikes midnight
Each hour descends to break into the slowest minute
You've ever known
Whilst each second takes you emotionally to a place
  unsignposted and unknown
A land where all are called (eventually), but
  unfortunately your invitation came a lot earlier and
  you don't believe it at this point
But until you've made it through
This place is now your own

It's the midnight grief club

Honey, emotionally, I'm home.

# Against Every Odd / Look At Us Now

*I wrote this on the Santa Monica beach sands eating a*
*Filet-O-Fish with extra tartare sauce with my*
*best friend.*

We learn lessons from every loss
When the world didn't and still doesn't understand
We became our own boss
Tied together from our earliest memory
With an almighty blessed knot

Being forced to understand life and its hurdles
After every shot
We reconfigured our minds
We rewrit the plot
We struggled for years to connect the dots
We became used to losing lots
But never us
We're enough after all,
We're all we got

It's very familiar
That our opinions are dissimilar
What a sight, when our thoughts collide
I guess that's our signature

But you best believe
When we do agree
If it's the world we're against
You're going to hear from him
And once you have heard from him
You're going to hear from me

# LIFE IS SAD & BEAUTIFUL

There was no rule book, no guide, no direction
For the road we travelled
Our buckles were loose,
Whilst numerous times we nearly fell from our saddles
Life had us in a headlock, powerless, emotionally
  rattled,
Psychologically tackled,
Through coping mechanisms and all we dabbled

Look at us now
Santa Monica Pier
Fish filet,
Smiling and laughing
At all we battled.

# £2

Two pounds would stretch a long way
Coming out from Mum's forever-enriching handbag
It was the ultimate way to brighten the day

That's five 20p sweets
With a whole one pound left
That could be saved for a rainy day
Or to be spent on an ice cream that would most likely
  dribble onto your chest

Two pounds would stretch a really long way
I miss the days
When the smaller amounts of money
From richer hands
Would enlighten me with a different beam of ray

Because, back in the day,
Two pounds would stretch a really long way.

# GRANDMA

She says I pray for you my baby,
Now make us a cup of tea
She says I pray for you my baby
That one day you will meet
Someone so lovely and together you'll make a family
She says I pray for you my baby,
That I'm there to see

I say I really love you Grandma
You've seen me grow and grow
And, at times, I'm far my Grandma,
There are things I don't wanna show,

Please don't ever leave me my grandma
The world is really cold, it's cold
I'm warm with you Grandma
For a moment I'm at home

I don't want a life without you,
I just want you to really know
I'm really trying my grandma
I'm really trying to hold on

We broke the rules my grandma
And some of us are really gone,
But just like you my grandma
I've learnt how to be strong

She says I pray for you my baby,
Now make us a cup of tea
She says I pray for you my baby
That one day you will meet

Someone so lovely and together you'll make a family
She says I pray for you my baby,
That I'm there to see

Don't you talk about you leaving
Cos if you go I'm coming too
Don't you talk about you leaving
That is really rude
Don't you talk about you leaving
That's not what you're meant to do
Don't talk about you leaving
Because I don't wanna be without you

No one prays for me my grandma,
From the heart like I know you do
I will never feel love again my grandma
Like I do when I'm next to you

She says I pray for you my baby,
Now make us a cup of tea
She says I pray for you my baby
That one day you will meet
Someone so lovely and together you'll make a family
She says I pray for you my baby,
That I'm there to see.

# YOU KNOW WHAT HE'S LIKE

Just take it
Brave it when you face it
We can't change it
You know what he's like

Not mindful
Spiteful
Pushes the dial
Lacks spinal
You know what he's like

Incomprehensible
Not very sensible
Undefendable
Nothing identical
You know what he's like

I used to question
The oppression
And aggression
Suppression and depression
How no progression
Is made in a life full of emotional congestion
Toxic DNA, that's become a profession
Internalised, unprocessed, compression
Rude expression
Demon possession

No,
You know what he's like
I don't want it or need it in my life.
You Know What I'm Like.

# Some Things Never Change

Some things never change
Because they're not meant to
Sometimes, some things stay in range
Because it's you who's meant to

Move
Choose
Not get an apology
Even though you did nothing wrong and it was you
Who got battered and bruised
Lose
Remove
Improve
Prove
You've
Approved
You

I tried to save you and that fault was mine
It must have been my ego mixed with an ounce of pride
I tried to make us be something we clearly wasn't,
  I lied
To convince myself we're doing fine

I mimed,
my gut was feeling multiple things but to my heart
  I would deny,
I cried
most nights about why you took so much of my time,
I hide
all of you I never want the world to know,
I ride

even though you don't deserve me by your side,
Jokes aside,
I let you convince me I was wrong, you was right,
besides
the motion in the gut,
I let you decide,
I'd glide, with all my might to swim against your tide
I implied
I didn't want to abide,
it amplified

When it was evident we wasn't unified,
I fried
the little love you supplied,
by my bedside on the East Side,
on the riverbank by the dockside,
I let you provide,

Things that were not clear whilst I sat ringside,
centre of my world you'd reside,
but I wasn't wishing it's in your arms I'd die,
because inside
I wasn't fine
I'm feeling the pressure of the shotgun
In this joyride
I replied
Try to untie
But was lost in the grass of the countryside
Without my compass

You was great to misguide
And, yeah, even though it was just my world
You flipped it for me worldwide
I didn't identify
The signs

I lowered my barrier of what it meant to feel
  dissatisfied

I'm overqualified
In feeling fine
I tried
But some things never change
Because they're not meant to
Some things stay in range
Because it's you who's meant to
Move
Choose
Not get an apology
Even though you did nothing wrong and it was you
Who got battered and bruised
Lose
Remove
Improve
Prove
You've
Approved
You

Because some things never change
They're not meant to
Sometimes, some things stay in range
Because it's you who's meant to
Move
Choose
Not get an apology
Even though you did nothing wrong and it was you
Who got battered and bruised
Lose
Remove

Improve
Prove
You've
Approved
You.

# TAKE CARE OF HER

Watching her leave the wedding hall
Was like watching your favourite main character leave
  the movie screen for the final time

Watching her depart in the car with our heart in your
  arms
Was a strikingly painful, melodic dream; one where we
  wiped tears from our eyes but was grateful we got to
  play our part

Provide her space if she requires
A home of her own if she ever desires
Patience when she fires
Brakes on the drive to complement the speed of her fast-
  paced tyres

Take care of her youth
Cherish her truth
Nurture her roots
Follow the steps of her boots
Embrace her extrovert
Comfort her recluse
Understand, but make no allowance for her excuse

Take care of her
Love her new
Love her true

Even through the most challenging of times

You find the words to tell her

I love you.

# Don't Worry, You Carry On

I'm not gonna lie, they're testing me
They're indirectly, directly affecting me
Not acknowledging my presence, but profoundly basically
 reflecting me
But they don't know what's in the vault in the clouds,
They have no idea what's protecting me.

# I ALWAYS CRY WHEN I HAVE TO SAY GOODBYE

I don't know what it is
Oh, who am I kidding? Of course I do
It's that time has gone too quick
That resembles into trembling in my bottom lip
It's waterworks
An ache that hurts
When you leaving me, is me loving you
But I'm smiling and hugging you
Knowing I have given all I can give

It's you downplaying the situation
It's me trying to pull it together
It's all within the atmosphere and the overwhelming
  sensation
Of footsteps increasing our distance
From here on ever

It's a song that's humming
It's our arguments of huffing and puffing
It's the butterflies that are blushing
The nights dancing and shuffling
The cheeks that expand whilst gushing
It's nothing that we are over-brushing
It's a love being forced to start rushing
It's instant minutes of pain and its crushing
It's two hearts parting that we are so great at becoming
Something from absolutely nothing
It's real friendship,
In the airport saying goodbye, that makes me cry,
It's stunning
The beats of my heart it's drumming

My strings it's tugging
My pain it's scrubbing
The hurt it's numbing
For all we had is not all we have
For all we have is transforming to who we are becoming

I always cry when I have to say goodbye
That's our love, loving.

# DON'T FALL ASLEEP AT THE WHEEL

There are only a few miles left
Even though it's not signposted
There are real friends to give you a hard shoulder to
  cry on
Just call them, stop thinking they've ghosted

Come on now, there are a only a few miles left
Keep your foot on the pedal
It's fine if you take the wrong exit,
  Just get back to the roundabout
It's completely normal that not every intersection or
  motorway will see you as special

Come on now,
Don't fall asleep at the wheel
Don't play songs that hurt your heart and stop it from
  having a moment to settle
Come on now, there are only a few miles left
Open the window
Get some fresh air to your face
Add some old-school garage
Pick up the treble

Did I see you smile?
Oh, you so cute,
You little rebel
Your smile is your medal

But I can't let you fall asleep at the wheel just yet
We're nearly there
When it gets harder don't reverse
Don't backpedal

It's fine you're sensitive
It's fine you're fragile
So are the edges of the white rose and its petals

Don't fall asleep at the wheel
You will hit road bumps, there are many unexpected
  hazards that just show up
Just recharge your battery,
Get the leads to jump

Get back on the road
And remember there are other places you can travel where
  you are loved.

# I Can't Wait

To walk down the stairs
And smell breakfast cooking
To trip over toys on the floor
Because I was walking and where I was going,
I wasn't looking

I can't wait to tell work
I can't attend today,
Because I have to be in attendance at your school
  assembly
And to me that is the most important booking

I can't wait to fall in love and build a home with you
And there's warmth when we walk on our floors
I can't wait to see the crayons and colours on the doors
The debates about scores
I can't wait to expand my heart
To wrap it around yours

For too long now,
I have been all alone
I can't wait
To meet you

I can't wait to make a home.

# BABY FEET

I hear baby feet
Running
Carrying the greatest
Of loving
Towards my bed
To wake my dreams of nothing
To a special smile of something
I hear baby feet
Running.

# THE WAVE IS COMING!

Balancing finely for dear life
On rubber rings that are inflatable
The sun beating
Through palm trees
Missing gaps in the teeth produce
The largest smiles
That haven't been seen in the longest while
An atmosphere sensational

Ah! The wave is coming
Using our hands to paddle down the sides of these rings
But merely no impact is made against the tidal
They are doing nothing
Can't risk the capsize by jumping off this double ring
In an attempt to be underwater running

Ah, too late

A high-pitched voice screams again

MAMMO, THE WAVE IS COMING!

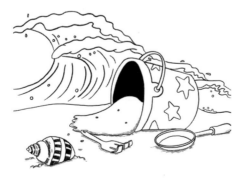

# It's Just One of the Things You Never Saw

I know they say you see everything
And a lot of people say
You have the best seat in the house
But what I'd like to know
Is are you actually watching us from where you're
 sitting
Because sometimes I really have a lot of doubt


Mum,
You have grandchildren now
Today we all went on a water slide
At first they cried and screamed
When the water went in their eyes
But after that they were running
Into the sunset, you should hear them fill the home with
 their noises when the sun rises
They went on the biggest slides multiple times,
 screaming 'I love you' as they weren't holding on tight!


They see a picture of your grave and they say Nanny
They hear us speak your name and they say Nanny


They see us wear the heaviest pain of grief, but we
 cover it with a smile because they don't deserve and
 you don't deserve for your legacy and their nanny to
 be ever known to be a difficult thing for us to carry


I bought the ride photos this time
I never cared for the price
The photographer captured a magical moment for life
I couldn't risk to not get it and hope one day for this

feeling to come twice

Mum, did you hear what I said?
I bought the ride photo this time
Because in my life I never got one with you by my side

We then hit the rapids
Intense for the kids
But, just like you, love the thrill of the fast life,
  the manic,
Water splashed
A quiet second
Will they cry?
Will they laugh?
Bit of both, ah magic!
Still eating dinner from greasy boxes will forever be
  teaching them ratchet lavish

I know they say you see everything
And a lot of people say
You have the best seat in the house
But what I'd like to know
Is are you actually watching us from where you're
  sitting
Because sometimes I really have a lot of doubt

They see a picture of your grave and they say Nanny
They hear us speak your name and they say Nanny

They see us wear the heaviest pain of grief, but we
  cover it with a smile because they don't deserve and
  you don't deserve for your legacy and their nanny to
  be ever known to be a difficult thing for us to carry.

# Even the Sky Cries

I don't like it when you hit yourself
I'm glad you've not done that in a while
Don't trip your health,
Don't go on a walk down that overthinking mile
That's not right
That's not nice

I need you to remember,
Even the sky cries

Don't overlap or cause harm to your memory
This feeling is just here for the interim whilst you
  adjust,
It's only temporary
Love is waiting for you
Loving, there will be plenty
You will be just fine

I need you to remember
Even the sky cries

I get it,
It's hard
It gets harder when it's lonely
When the place you thought was home
But now no essence of it feels homely
And there's not much left in you that can fight

I just need you to remember
Even the sky cries
You keep telling yourself
This ain't you

You're stronger than this
You can't believe it
But look, it's happened and we're here
You put your love where it wasn't met
I know, first hand, that's not nice

Which is why I really need you to remember

Even the sky cries
Even the sky cries
Even the sky cries

I just need you to remember

Even the sky cries.

# HEY LITTLE MAN

Hey little man
Do you know how to wipe your tears from your mind?
You find a place you can go
A space that not many know
Where there are only kind things you find
Because if you sit in the darkness long enough,
Eventually the sun will rise

Hey little man
Do you know how to install the peace amongst the land of
  the things you deep?
When there's so much going on
Try to get comfortable in the night
Even when it gives you a fright
Because if you sit in the darkness long enough,
Eventually the sun will rise

Hey little man
You can't flourish
If you punish
All of what you're meant to nourish
That's not how you're meant to get by
You really have to trust
You really can't give up
Because if you sit in the darkness long enough
Eventually the sun will rise

Hey little man
What are you doing?
Why are you being so horrible?
You must treat yourself honourable
This behaviour is not tolerable

I thought we'd already discussed this tonight
That if you sit in the darkness long enough
Eventually the sun will rise

And believe it will
And when it does
It will smile at you to be with you
Its rays will calm your senses to help breathe with you
To help find and seek with you
It's not there to patronise
It's there to be with you

Because if you sit in the darkness long enough
Eventually the sun will rise

You can't lie or act surprised
It's one thing the darkness hitting you
But it's a completely different thing when the sun hits back

Because if you sit in the darkness long enough
Eventually the sun will rise

Hey little man
What do we call this one?

'I think we call it, "Hey Little Man"'

Sounds about right, little man, sounds about right.

# From Me to You from Malibu

The waves are chaotic
But they're calming
They hit your head
But it's not like a pain or a trauma
Something about that sudden impact is refreshingly,
   dangerously charming

The sky becomes a blanket
With its reds, pinks, purples,
In its confusion it's disarming
Shh,
You can hear the birds call,
In an attempt to find their nest
Lost
Mixed with washed human footprints in the sand,
Away from home but their call is never alarming

To my loves,
Who hold a piece of my heart
I give all of what's in me
To all of what's in you
In an attempt that the tears from my tide touch the
   centre of your palm
From what's left in me
To what's inside of you
From the Pacific Coast Highway
Here in Malibu

I believe Ammi Jaan is in Heaven
Under Heaven's lights
And if this is where my tides have turned
I have no idea how I will be able to comprehend the

beauty of what Heaven's like
But I'll do my best to get to Heaven right

Shh,
Relax, it will be all right
Because in Malibu
When the dark sets sight
The peace of the night sets flight

Eventually, the temperature
The mood becomes suitable
Regardless of where we set foot on this earth,
Life will always be sad
But life will always be beautiful.

# If California

If California was a dream
I'd hold her in my heart
I'd let her warmth comfort my bruises
I'd let my tears fall and be caught in her art

If California was a highway
I'd overstay my welcome in her intersection
I'd park somewhere quiet to watch her sunset
I'd sit smiling in her traffic east to west without
    taking any of the locals' suggestions

If California was a pier
I'd brush away the clouds that cause her fog
I'd promise her the sun will break through and we'll get
    the time back for the time we lost

If California was an ocean
I would never complain
I'd listen to her waves
How each one, eloquent, majestic, demanding
Her water is never the same

If California was a boulevard
I'd save her the pain of listening to my dreams
I'd fill the gaps in the cracks
In an attempt to show her my intentions are clean

If California was a mother
She'd carry her child firm across the sands
If California was a father
He'd lead with passion as his plan

# THE BEAUTY AND THE PEACE

If California was a time
If California was a place
If California could ever be mine
I'd hope to find my place.

# Wet Play in California

From the City to the Valley
Nobody wants to play outside
When it's raining in Cali.

# Postcard

I don't wish you were here
I wish I was there
Around you lot, smiling and grinning
Those who can see I'm still trying to lose weight
Those who can see my hair is thinning
But tell me don't worry
We got a good angle
So we'll get the picture from over here
I'm losing my mind too early
But momentarily around you lot everything in this place
  I'm feeling makes me feel like I'm winning

I don't wish you were here
I wish I was there
To sing happy happy birthday the moment I see the cake
  being brought out at the heights of my voice,
So everyone sitting around us feels us celebrating your
  incredible life, your joy

I don't wish you were here
I wish I was there
And I wish I didn't have to make a choice

Between you all and my hand luggage and a poetic dream
That's torn, I'm attempting to re-stitch it at its fine
  line at the kameez's seams
Whilst I'm globe-trotting, soul-searching
On my mission, attempting to achieve
Convincing the world a broken light can still and has
  every right to beam
I don't wish you were here
I wish I was there

But it calms me knowing
We've qualified past the stage of friendship where we
   can truly pick up
Where we left off because we are the realest team

I've sacrificed your weddings,
Birthdays, moments of greatness
I just hope the photo still captures my presence and you
   can all forgive me
Because you know I can't do this without your grace and
   patience
But I have to head to the departure gate with all these
   feelings the Lord gave me

Sometimes these feelings really hit hard
So I really don't wish you were here
I wish I was there
Happy Birthday 31st S. P.!
I had to write you a postcard x

PS I hope they sang!

# MY DAY ONES

When my life tried
When my love dried
They're my day ones, my real friends,
They moved closer to me when I cried

Didn't bat an eye
Or hesitate to walk by
Didn't leave even though I gave plenty of good enough
  reasons for them to hit me a goodbye
They sat tight
Didn't force me,
But let me decide
Became an extended family of mine

To fix it at home I tried
I tried and tried
And I sit in my container every night
I pray with might
It will be all right

My day ones,

When my life tried
When my love dried
They're my day ones, my real friends,
They moved closer to me when I cried

To myself I became damaging
I'd disappear in my Yaris, surprised I never wrote a
  poem called 'Vanishing'
Overwhelming myself, panicking

My hearts way too fragile for this thing called life and
  that wasn't clear on the packaging

My day ones,
When my life tried
When my love dried
They're my day ones, my real friends,
They moved closer to me when I cried
Became an extended family of mine.

# I'M HOMESICK

I miss the pointless drives on endless highs whilst
  floating through local skies

I'm homesick

I miss the samosa from Father
The antics, the drama
The way we laugh harder
McDonald's drive thru in our old-school pyjamas

I'm homesick

I miss the lack of motives
How everyone's showbiz
The energy's explosive
Someone's always got something they're promoting

I'm homesick

I miss the conversations coming home from the train
  stations about how we never successfully passed any
  application, but my generation is still determined to
  change the law of nations, through our own cultural
  declaration, don't worry about managing me, you just
  focus on managing your own expectations,

I miss the mehndis, the walimas, the celebrations,
The days of music of Avril Lavigne, 'Sk8er Boi' and the
  complications

I miss the Muhammad Ali activism in multiple
  combinations

I'm homesick

Of a world I once knew that has now sunk quick
To a place I can't recognise and I feel suffocated by
 the apps, the data,
I'm still waiting for an anthropologist or sociologist
 to write a theory on being virtually consumed and
 digitally claustrophobic

I miss the pointless drives on endless highs whilst
 floating through local skies

I'm homesick

I miss the samosa from Father
The antics, the drama
The way we laugh harder
McDonald's drive thru in our old-school pyjamas

I'm homesick

I miss the lack of motives
How everyone's showbiz
The energy's explosive
Someone's always got something they're promoting

I'm homesick.

# Go Home!

If you dabble in a world that's not meant for you
You will attract the spirits that don't care for you
They'll lead you astray and never will they stay
Until the moment you need someone to be there for you

It starts with the mispronunciation of my name with no
   attempt to respect its cultural heritage

That tells me, there's a frustration within your frame
   that, by default, you select with your display of
   disrespectful messaging

There's an undertone of bother, hatred and animosity
When having to deal with me, my brother, my sister,
   father and mother,
That you proudly wear constantly, consciously, commonly

When flying,
They don't tell you,
If you look like this,
You have to mentally manage the baggage, of the package
   you package that's soon to be internally damaged by a
   uniform savaged on the journey of your peaceful passage

Which is why I will never grow accustomed
To how I am treated at customs
For the custom
For you are fully aware of the mental warfare and
   intimidation strategy you push in order to cause those
   who you deem to look outcasted a form of psychological
   conundrum,
Daily in the hundreds

# THE BEAUTY AND THE PEACE

It starts when you're the only one who looks like you
And your workplace becomes a dungeon,
When allyship is performative
And truthfully you're really outnumbered
It's really not that deep, to want to live and let
  peace, I've wondered

Our generation is not naive in thinking we can lift the
  bar
Believe me, I know it's a heavy weight, and I'll spot
  you, cos I got you,
And if discrimination is taking you to the darkness,
  just know one thing
It's in the darkness we find stars,

I just wish 2022 becomes the year,
We begin to change, check and correct our DNA,
And we truly give through how we live
With who we truly are.

# IT'S 3AM IN E2

*Oi, hurry up and open the door, I'm pressing the buzzer.*

Balcony river spots
Highlights all the shots
Pure intention the whole gang has got
It's 3am in E2
And all of us have just lost the plot.

# SIBLINGS

You all remind me of mum
We talk, we fight, we shout, that's us
You're in the right, someone's in the wrong
It's ok, let's not fight, let's just show more trust
We all miss mum
We all love dad

We all are our love

# Help Me Pick a Baby Name :)

I cried when you told me
The tears just fell
I don't care for anything from this point
Just both of your health and happiness
And that heavenly, angel, baby smell
I'm emotional
More than usual
You can tell
I can't believe it

'OK, but do you have any name suggestions?'

I've always loved Yahya,
Yakub or Zakariya,

You know your baby will have the best uncle in the world
  right?
'Yeah, OK'

I wish mum was here to see,
'Yeah, same'

Outro

# Your Emotions Deserve to Be Given the Time of Day

Well, what a journey this has been. I never actually
felt like this day would come. But after writing poetry
for 17 years it eventually did. I'm not sure during
which time period of my life I learnt the following, but
it must have been relatively early or it just made sense
from the offset. And that was that I must always honour
my emotions in the time I am given them.

For me that's more than a sentence - it's a
statement, a code of conduct, a lifelong partnership I
have developed with myself. The moment I feel something,
I must act on it, sit down in it, with it, breathe life
into it, write about it, speak about it and develop a
piece from it. But there is a fine balance to getting
it right. I can't overstay my welcome in my own head,
heart or mind; I can't overfeed a gut feeling, an
inkling or a hunch. I must get the formula correct in
order to deal with it with the necessary accordance.
Failure to do so can result in disastrous mental
catastrophes, such as depressed overthinking and cynical
clinical anxiety.

We all know too well that emotions send absolutely
no warning signs before they show up - emotional
triggers are constantly finding new ways of reinventing
themselves once you have developed internal growth. And
therefore it makes it even more significant for me that
the time given is the time when the emotion must be
dealt with.

This basically means that it does not matter where I
am, who I am with or what time of day or night it is, if
I feel something, I must write about it. I pull out my
pen and paper and I begin.

I have lost many nights of sleep due to waking
up from a dream that has inspired a piece. I have
been absent-minded around the people who make me feel

truly loved because an emotion decided to appear in
the forefront of my mind, attempting to occupy the
space, and I had to court it in my heart to really
understand where it had come from, why it came and, most
importantly, what I was meant to learn from it.

I truly have learnt to view emotions as a spiritual
gift sent from a divine power that enables us to connect
on a level that is remarkable and beautiful, but only
if we let them. The chance of being open, honest and
vulnerable to yourself is a blessing; it's an incredible
experience that defines us as humans and ultimately
leads to a form of social emotional learning.

Something we must never stop doing is learning,
especially about ourselves. The moment we do, we enter
dangerous territory. But also when we believe we truly
know it all and don't pay our mind, emotions or our
internal DNA the time they truly deserve, I really do
believe we begin to suppress how we are feeling and this
is an ultimate red flag.

Emotions that are suppressed lead to internal
punishment, toxic treatment of yourself by yourself and
an unhappy life. It's really very difficult initially to
develop a pattern of owning the emotions you are gifted
with, but once you have started you will only thank
yourself for it.

We as the world have experienced a magnitude and
multitude of historical changes throughout our time
period alone. Now more than ever we must take the time
for ourselves and for each other to really put ourselves
in a position of emotional stability in order to thrive
through life.

I recently went to Paris and, for the first time
in my life, I laid my eyes on the Eiffel Tower and I
started crying. I was overwhelmed - and you can really

absorb the complexities of what was created that night
in the piece 'Fridge Magnets'.

The poems in this book were created at various
stages of my life throughout various parts of the
world I was exceptionally fortunate to travel to. For
me, I have never really found the term 'poem' to do
them justice; they are pieces of my heart, my life, my
absolutely everything and at the same time they are,
actually, nothing.

*Life Is Sad and Beautiful* was created from the
mountains of Bogotá, Colombia, the hills of Kashmir,
by the waters of Mangla Dam, in the bustle of the
Lahore markets, the traffic of Bangkok, by the side of
the beauty of Koh Phi Phi, the all-inclusive hotel in
Magaluf, the culture of Paris, the peaceful isolation
of Normandy, the desert sands of the Middle East, the
holy land of Saudi Arabia, the peaceful bliss submerged
within the nights of Medina, the beach house of Santa
Monica, the white little bungalow in Malibu, the forest
drives of Austria, the family trips to Margate, the
road trips across the States from Washington to Florida
to Colorado to New York City, the long drives through
Essex looking at houses we can't afford, the mighty
ship that carried me through Niagara Falls, the castle
of Ottawa in Canada, the Atlas Mountains of Morocco,
the mighty Mount Kilimanjaro, the bed and breakfast
in Fort William, Scotland, the fish markets in Cape
Town, the refugee camps of Europe, the clear skies of
Palm Springs, the majestic sunsets of Botswana and the
mighty Belgrave Road; it was created across 15 notepads,
my school planners and countless mobile phones; it
was created with tears coming down my face and smiles
beaming from my big mouth; it was created at open mic
nights in East London (brap brap!), Trinity Buoy Wharf

and at the Original Emotion Picture Studios, but out of everywhere I have travelled, the most peaceful, blissful place I have ever written in was within the walls of the loving home of my dearest mother, the legendary garden shed she created for us and that small box room where 'Lyrical Gangsta' was born.

I will leave you now with my final piece, it's called:

'For When It's My Time'

The biggest gift my mother left us was her constant reminder of what to do when she is no longer here, which was to 'cry and get over it'. Many people I know avoid the conversation of death; I don't, not anymore. We must be warm to it. We must let our loved ones know the instructions of how we wish them to carry out our funeral preparations, our legacy, but, most importantly, how we want them to heal through this heartbreaking heartbreak. The five words she left us with are enough to get me through this time.

Which is why I decided to write this piece - drum roll please ... this is it. Oh, wait, one last thing:

I really have learnt life is sad, but, and yes there
is a but,
if you keep going,
if you work on yourself, your mind and your love
if you never give up,
your life, too, can be beautiful.

# For When It's My Time

Take a moment to send a prayer to the sky
To help lift my aching soul as it takes its flight
To paradise
For this happens to be my time

Smile for every time,
My big mouth spoke truth in rooms
It was not meant to be inside
I ensured our point got across,
The planets did collide
This just happens to be my time

Eagerly take steps to the side
By my grave in line
To allow my questioning to begin
And my answers no longer need to rhyme
This just happens to be my time

Take comfort my baby nephew
And darling niece
It will all be all right
I'm with my mummy now,
I've waited an entire life
This just happens to be my time

I hope to love you again
Where it's so true
There's no need to read between the lines
As this truly is
I will see you again, real soon
This is the furthest thing from a goodbye

It just happens to be my time.

Keep going,
Keep fighting,
Keep writing,
Keep rhyming,

And always remember

To cry and get over it.

Hussain Manawer
The Original Mummy's Boy

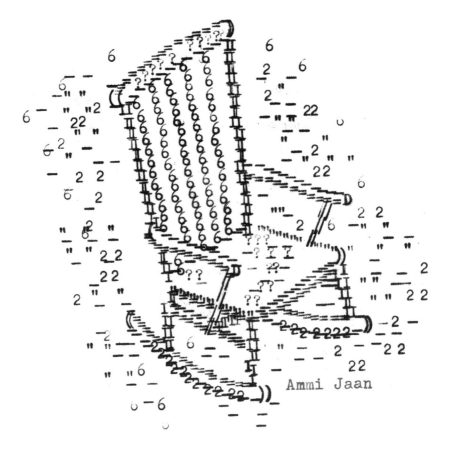

Ammi Jaan

# About the Author

From my mum

I told my son to always brush his teeth before he goes to bed, because the world is going to see him smile. He always spills food on his clothes and would never sleep if we were going somewhere exciting the next day, so I wouldn't tell him. And just like me, he loves a vegetable samosa with mint chutney.

He is a mummy's boy, he is my baby, and he is saved in my phone as my King. I was proud of him when he graduated. Whenever he would travel, I would message him and tell him the house was quiet without him and I would get him mangos and watermelons for his return.

When he won the trip to Space, I was happy, everyone was, but I never wanted him to go. I said if something happened to him in space, I wouldn't be able to help him.

I remember one day he was sad in the grey room on the sofa, and he said he felt like giving up on his career, I told him, not to worry because I pray with a clean heart and God listens to those who do. He said, it's too hard, there's too much competition, and I replied.

'God says if you got it, you must feed the world and that is exactly what we will be doing, you get it, and quietly we will feed the world, so just let them copy you, just don't get stressed over it.'

yellow
kite

books to help you live a good life

Join the conversation and tell
us how you live a #goodlife

@yellowkitebooks
YellowKiteBooks
Yellow Kite Books
YellowKiteBooks